A LIFE IN PIECES

*A Piece-by-Piece Guide to Realizing Harmony
in Families, Schools, and Communities*

A LIFE IN PIECES

*A Piece-by-Piece Guide to Realizing Harmony
in Families, Schools, and Communities*

by

Lana Buoy

DORRANCE PUBLISHING CO., INC.
PITTSBURGH, PENNSYLVANIA 15222

ISBN: 978-0-8059-7619-9

Printed in the United States of America

First Printing

For more information or to order additional books, please contact:
Dorrance Publishing Co., Inc.
701 Smithfield Street
Third Floor
Pittsburgh, Pennsylvania 15222
U.S.A.
1-800-788-7654
www.dorrancebookstore.com

This book is dedicated to all children through a message of love:

I am living my heaven on earth, rejoicing in your spirit.
I want you to know that you opened my darkness, bit by bit.

Your humility and simplicity, your energy and curiosity,
Rebounded me into a life that is pleasing and witty.

I dream of peace built by children who possess divine virtue
and grace.
A child's mind is free of bias and complications, revealing a most
accepting face.

I am sad to have missed many years genuinely experiencing life.
Now I thrive in your attempt to live "as one," without heartache
and strife.

Children, you are kind, warm and concerned for others; you bring
me joy.
I want peace to engulf the souls of every girl and boy.

I vow never to forget your valuable spirit and personality.
You have allowed me to live with much rationality.

Thank you, from the bottom of my heart.

CONTENTS

I AM GOOD
I AM NOT BAD

I AM EAGER
I AM NOT DISRESPECTFUL

I AM CHEERFUL
 I AM NOT RESENTFUL

I AM A FRIEND AND PARTNER
I AM NOT UNSUPPORTIVE

I AM FAIR
I AM NOT BIASED

I AM BRIGHT
I AM NOT ANGRY OR VENGEFUL

I AM HAPPY
I AM NOT ANNOYING

I AM LOVE
I AM NOT MEAN OR MALICIOUS

I AM WANT
I AM NOT SELFISHLY NEEDY

I AM ABLE TO CHOOSE
I AM NOT UN-COOPERATIVE

I AM CAPABLE OF COMMUNICATING AND I WANT TO
TALK.
I AM NOT HYPER (in a "bad" way) OR DISRUPTIVE

I AM A HELPER
I AM NOT SELF-CENTERED OR UNFEELING

I AM ABLE TO REMEMBER
I AM NOT FORGETFUL

I AM BEAUTY

ACKNOWLEDGMENTS

It is important for me to thank the people who have been a part of the task of completing this book. The following thanks comes from deep within my heart.

I thank all my friends, co-workers, and family who have been excited about, and supportive of this journey. We share the realization that the world is desperate for genuine transformation. We have grown together in spirit, both emotionally and intellectually, as we share the desire for peace and the sadness in its absence. We have lost our ignorance and innocence, as we no longer shut out the tragic truths of the world. It is this that fuels the search for genuine peace.

To all my workshop participants thus far, your intense concentration regarding this solution to peace is empowering. Your willingness to listen to a revolutionary process calms my heart, as you have proven there are adults who humbly accept that some old beliefs may be ready for retirement and new approaches can be implemented, especially ones that ensure the safety of all children. Thank you for your words of encouragement, as they inspire me. I promise you, as you have asked, that I will not give up the fight to bring a more gentle approach to raising our children. It is this that can make change a reality and the world truly humanitarian.

To Michelle, we had a connection from our very first phone conversation as we discussed the ideals of *A Life in Pieces*. From then on, I gained a new friend.

A special thanks to my one and only employee, my dad, who created an awesome puzzle that has changed the lives of many children and adults. I brought a drawing on a napkin to your dining room table in April 2004 and asked if this could be created into a tangible puzzle from which children and adults could see, touch, and learn.

From the years that have followed, you built and refined wood until the *A Life in Pieces* puzzle shone like gold before my eyes. We now share a unique relationship and I am very fortunate to have you with me. Your belief in the beauty of this program is evident in every piece of the numerous puzzles you have built.

To Chris, what would life be like if we had never met for coffee fourteen years ago? I dare say there are few friends who can visit weekly for so many years and still have hours of conversation left and ready for the next week. You are my soulmate, as we share the same feelings and thoughts, first in regards to motherhood and now to the world. I came across a life partner, and I shall never lose you. You have made my journey.

The greatest gratitude of all goes to the four people who have been in the presence of this program since its inception: my husband and three children. I could write a book expressing my love and thanks, as there is so much to say. I want to exclaim that I am filled with joy to have you, Brian, loving, creating, and growing with me in understanding as we journey through our life in pieces. There are not too many husbands willing to venture into such a daunting experience, but thankfully you have, as it changed our life. I am unable to describe what you, Amie, Curtis, and Mallorie, have done for me, as my feelings transcend any definition in the English language. You touch the very depths of my soul. I never dreamed love could feel this way. Thank you for letting me experience this.

INTRODUCTION

Welcome to "A Life in Pieces: a Piece-by-Piece Guide to Realizing Harmony in Families, Schools and Communities." Enjoy this unique process that can eliminate obstacles interfering with the cultivation of peace. "A Life in Pieces" begins by intensifying the genuine, innate goodness and exemplified spirit of a newborn. Through repeated affirmations exclaiming "I am all I need to be," this beauty continues as the child matures gracefully into a humble adult, possessing strength in humility and simplicity. When the time comes, this unpretentious adult is eager to welcome his/her newborn, who like its parent, possesses genuine innate goodness and exemplified spirit....

the cycle continues....

CHAPTER ONE

A LIFE OF BEAUTY FOR ALL

Imagine a helpless, confused child stands alone in fear, longing for a moment that may never come—a time when the people in her life are more loving and calm, with a desire to understand the pieces of her life, her mind, and her soul. This child prays that her parents, teachers, and members of her extended family and community will come to appreciate the truth—that she is a curious child with feelings and emotions that need to be expressed. She questions why adults are dissatisfied and irritated in, and seemingly by, her presence, and the presence of many children around her. She is getting increasingly frustrated with adults misinterpreting her actions and thinking she is bad. All she is trying to do is please those around her. This causes moments of extreme anxiety, and it is then that she wishes to scream, "I am not bad!" She becomes desperate, as impossible moral and emotional expectations are placed upon her; more so than any adult would place on themselves. What is most distressing is that her attempts to explain this confusion seem to be unheard, or worse, are seen as intentionally oppositional and cause the adults in her life to call her names that describe a devil child, someone impossible to live with. This child feels confused and helpless. To her, the spirit that imbues her heart intensifies the truth that she is all she needs to be, respectfully and morally. To her, she is lovable. To me, she is only a child, one longing for a peaceful life.

Imagine this same child glowing in happiness, thankful to be in the presence of grown-ups who have, since her birth, found joy in the inherent virtues that radiate from the very depths of her spirit. This child's parents, extended family, teachers and community have repeatedly affirmed that she is filled with goodness. This gives comfort to the child as she lives the kind of life she rightfully deserves—one that is filled with equality and love to make her happy, and also rambunctious curiosity and energy to help her learn. This positive treatment by the grown-ups in her life creates, for her, a vision of the adult she will become: a socially developed, morally productive humanitarian, who herself will be free and willing to affirm the innate virtues of the children she will meet, thus allowing them a chance to thrive in present and future relationships. This young life is full of genuine euphoria, the natural result of growing in a positive environment. This is beauty, as everyone around her realizes she is all she needs to be. To her, she is lovable and she is loved. To the world, she exudes peace. To me, she is only a child, one ready to thrive in a compassionate world.

The developing contrast of this child's two lives is the result of polarized interpretations of universal truths regarding the steps needed to achieve genuine humanity and peace. The first life of this child concentrates on the child-rearing philosophy that suggests the steps to peaceful relationships are achieved through the controlling intervention of grown-ups who feel they must train children to become moral and productive adults. This philosophy torments the child, as she is perceived as lacking what is required to thrive and survive in this world, thus creating tense connections with adults who watch her every move, ensuring everything she does is right by their interpretation. This child does not dare to stray away from the respect expected of her by, and towards, grown-ups. Sadly, this child comes to understand feelings of hypocrisy while living with people who ask of her what they would not ask of themselves. It grows increasingly difficult to live in a relationship where respect is not returned. As this hypocrisy builds, so does the child's feelings of humiliation and insult. Life for this child becomes bleak, with possibilities that she will grow depressed, angry, violent, and/or emotionally illiterate. These are just a few of the consequences resulting from inequality in relationships and the suppression of feelings and emotions related to injustice.

The contrary life of this child, who is glowing in purity and perfection, allows her to grow into an adult whose spirit remains intact. Nurturing her innate virtues takes her to a utopia of safety, freeing her from emotions which cause frustration and anxiety. She is then allowed to grow into a self-realized adult who has internalized the true meaning of moral excellence and respect. This emotional stability breeds acceptance of those around her, despite diversity of religion, culture, age or gender. This is the path to her genuine humanity. This is the path to world humanity, a concept materialized through a peace process I want to share.

Readers, I share this concept with ease. It has become natural for me to speak words of virtue, shared by all of mankind, through a process that will become natural for you as well. If world humanity is to be achieved, then people in the world must find what it is they can share happily and equally as a collective group. Words, and the experience felt within when intensifying the meaning of each word, are used the world over. Therefore, it is through a deep investigation of words, such as kind, bright and fair, that humans can come to live harmoniously and happily. I am excited to begin the journey to humanity, not with the whole world, but with each person who reads and adapts his/her life to the intense, yet simple guide that is "A Life in Pieces." As this guide becomes clear to one individual, it will grow from him/her to others, allowing its beauty to permeate into the hearts of more adults and children. I rejoice in the opportunity to share what I have learned living through the eyes and heart of a child, something that has reawakened the feelings and emotions I experienced as a child. It is these experiences that inspired me to define and compare two contrary lives, using contrary words to describe the character of one child. The feeling of hopelessness I get when writing and reading about the life of a child who is "bad" (one of the many words I feel are misused), led me to cement my commitment to as many children as possible, helping to free them from a life of despair. My heartfelt goal is to lead them to a life of love and beauty, two words of hope integrated into the languages of the world. We must start to define and investigate these terms, to feel them and use them with intensity. A life of hope and happiness for a child is a life of spiritual prosperity. This prosperity, developed through the positive consequences of affirming beauty in the soul of all people, will grow into global humanity. I affirm this with ease.

The conclusion is that we are all we need to be. The simplicity of my conclusion, using words that show the belief in, and exaltation of, the innate virtues existing in all humans from conception, leads me to ponder how and why we continue to fail in our humanitarian obligation. It is so simple to say and believe that, morally and righteously, we are all we need to be. I also ponder humanity's continued inaction, or use of inappropriate actions, when the increase in hurt and torment in the world screams a dire need for change in thought and behavior towards all humans. I reflect upon the increase in abuse and bullying toward children by adults when it is so simple to affirm, "You are kind." It is impossible to abuse with such an affirmation. We must take to heart why so many women are abused and treated unfairly when calm arises with affirmations like, "You are bright; you are a great person." I sit, anxiously waiting to end my questions and confusion with the affirmation accepted by, and calming to, many people in this world, "We are all children of a higher, grander being." It is that simple. Because we have been created by one greater in spirit than any human, we are all we need to be, at the first sign of life.

I know it is simple and possible to realize a complete shift in thinking and belief because I have experienced this. What do others believe? Is it possible to change thoughts that have been imbedded in the mind for so long? How does one begin the process of change and can it go so far as to achieve success in equality for every man, woman, boy, and girl? Where and how do we begin to achieve this goal of lasting, genuine equality and peace? I believe it is at the inception of a new life, when one is free to begin anew, free to believe anything. Imagine....

You receive the joyous news that you are about to give birth to an event that will change your life. The event can be a new baby, a new job or promotion, a new relationship, and/or a new country. The birth of a baby can be a powerful event, with the greatest impact on your heart and mind that one can experience. The idea of a new job can be exciting. It may come after years of study, or years of hard work to further your professional and personal life. The progression of a dating relationship growing to a marriage is hopeful as you commit wholeheartedly to each other. A new life for an immigrant in a strange country can be daunting, as he/she envisions a new culture and people who will hopefully show respect, compassion and understanding. No matter the event that changes a life, it comes with responsibilities and the unknown, inevitably creating times of worry and questions. What do you believe the outcome will be? What are your beliefs based on? Your future and past will affect your vision of this new experience. For example, you may sense that the pieces of your past may affect your ability to successfully parent a child that you are bringing into an imperfect world; respect and work with the views of new co-workers and employer; embrace the values and personality of your new lifetime partner; and/or integrate to a life of different ideals and customs. You question how all the life-time knowledge thus far will affect your ability to succeed. You question the need for change, and you may be challenged to push beyond the question and pursue a complete paradigm shift. The pieces of your new life now sit before you.

Calm your heart and mind as I guide you through the birth and process of "A Life in Pieces." You will see that hope can be present in the life you live now and in the new beginnings that may be your future. There are easy solutions to personal success and happiness, and I will tell you what they are. So, get yourself ready because beauty and enlightenment are waiting to explode. Begin to work toward the successful inclusion of goodwill. Understand that you can put your fears of a forever volatile relationship, unhappy employment, or even an imperfect world, to rest. You can partake in a process that will solidify the fact that love and compassion are the basis of all peaceful relationships. Start a lesson in humility with "A Life in Pieces," and be willing to change your life for the better.

"I am all I need to be. I am kind. I am bright. I am beauty."

Begin now, and continue forever, to explore and affirm these phrases and many more. You will come to understand why it is that you not only deserve, but actually will, come to live in peace.

CHAPTER TWO

THE BEAUTY IN MY LIFE: THE AWAKENING

Parents, educators, husbands, wives, grandparents and anyone else in this world surviving the trials and tribulations of relationships, I am ready to begin our journey into the depths of very special words. Through a detailed investigation of the definition of each word, I will communicate my picture of the beauty hidden in the soul of every "child," both young and old. It is important to clarify my implication of the word child because I feel it embraces not just persons aged newborn to twenty one, but also those beyond legal age. I share information to support my realization that innate goodness like kindness, and emotions such as eagerness and curiosity, are with us from the day of conception to the day we die. I am concentrating my message on this important fact, because it is easier for adults to empathize and sympathize with children when they compare the identical emotions and feelings that live in the heart of children to those that survive in their own heart. This creates a natural response of adjusting the ways in which we as adults interpret (or misinterpret) the actions and behaviors of children, and ultimately how we treat them; the change has begun. I share how an adult's misinterpretation of children's outward emotional displays and behaviors (for example "opposition") can destroy character and change personality because, to children, it is the intent instigated by their state of mind and feeling inside their heart that has been misjudged, not the act itself. For example, an act interpreted as deviant, but intended to be justified and innocent will be insulting and confusing to a child. The misinterpretation of intentions, no matter what they are, can lead to emotions that negatively affect who a child becomes as an adult.

It is through this enlightenment that I reveal the solution for peace: the true understanding of our children, which will decrease anxiety and desperation, thus allowing calmer hearts, more joyful relationships and safer environments. All this beauty leads to the emotional stability needed within our psyche to solidify calm and assure equality. Enjoy this enlightenment through feelings and emotions expressed in "A Life in Pieces" that permit a different way of life; one that is more pleasing and successful. Readers, grow in peace as you retrieve your childhood spirit, love, curiosity, compromise and just treatment. Learn to empathize with all children.

It is my need for conscience cleansing that I communicate to, and about, the children I have had contact with throughout my life. I have learned many lessons comparing the two contrary lives of both children and adults, and while progressing through the process of redemption, I changed my life philosophy. I share the lesson that created a paradox—solidifying my truth that every human possesses innate virtues (to be intensified from birth), thus allowing for the fair and cooperative relationships we all strive for. The greatest truth arising from this contrary approach to training our children into perfected adults, is the reduction, if not the elimination, of frustration and anxiety that can arise from virtue training that expects too much. The phrase, "I expect you children to be good and kind today when we go to Grandma's house, and if you are not you will have consequences," is replaced with, "Children, you are kind and respectful, so I know we will have a beautiful visit at Grandmas." The anxiety felt by the grown-up caused by the expectation, and possible lack, of certain behaviors is eliminated because the children are kind and considerate, concerned for Grandma, and wanting to make the visit pleasant for everyone. There is no worry that the children will be rude or disrespectful, therefore the goal of a peaceful visit is assumed a success even before they go.

This lesson in humility, which was letting go of unfair expectations and control, cleansed my spirit and opened my mind to produce a much wiser "me." I have come to diversify my existence in this world and the role I will play while I am alive. I no longer concentrate on just my title of "happy wife and mother," carrying the responsibility to love and support my husband and three children. I now highlight the title of "employee," someone needing to be compassionate and cooperative with fellow-employees and my employer; "educator," someone needing to be wise, empathetic and fair to my students; "friend," someone needing to be supportive and sympathetic; and "human being," someone needing to be passionate, simple-minded, unoffended in my need for change, and unafraid to pass on this solution to peace. Join me in these diverse roles and see how this can bring you closer to realizing true happiness and lasting peace.

I must first gain your trust as I lead you to wander away from sacred child-rearing philosophies and techniques that include the adult's belief that it is they who need to train children to be righteous and courteous beings. I start with my enlightenment and new beginning that came unexpectedly twelve years ago and continues still today. Twelve years ago despair crept into my life and created, for me, a completely different understanding of what I thought life, particularly family, was, and is about. In a time of helplessness, my greatest hurt, surprise, and confusion came with the truth that immediate family members were willing to express openly hostile emotions and attitudes, including bias, inequality, misinterpretation, dislike and even contempt. Due to this realization, felt deep within my soul, I came to envision, and feel, a sad new reality that woke me to the agony felt by children experiencing despair due to injustice. As a result, my life has now changed. I speak truths discovered through my unexpected new beginning to life. One truth stands out: if I cannot live safely and happily in such conditions, a child cannot either.

Hopelessness and helplessness festered inside my soul as situations around me worsened. But, instead of killing my spirit, these feelings came to empower and enlighten me. I became aware of the unseen feelings that existed inside the recesses of my heart and mind. This propelled me into action, and I worked endlessly and full-heartedly to find a solution to end these traumatizing realities, as trauma disallows the presence of peace and happiness. It is times like these that the fight existing within ourselves, which I call our "innocence and purity," screams out for those around to stop the humiliating and insulting injustice, as it affects how one feels and behaves. If the strong rejections felt within the heart go unheard (as in my case) or are punished, anxiety will build and adrenaline rules much of what one does. It is hard to sit, think, remember, or to be happy. But, if the feelings felt from within can be expressed and heard, strength builds and the injustice weakens. Because of the personal experiences I had with continuous acts of injustice that caused confusion, anxiety, and devastation, I am now able to share what some children go through: the feeling of desperation. At the time I was most desperate, my innocence and purity, or my invisible protector, allowed me the strength and courage to scream for change that would create respect and kindness, the very character traits expected of children. It is ironic that these values were absent in some of the adults in my life, the ones who claimed to have passed the moral-skills training, professing to treat all compassionately and equally. Did the training fail? Did they forget everything they were trained to do and say? The truth is neither, but that virtues can be intensified; they cannot be taught or trained. It is this truth that empowered me to find a solution for peace.

In order to bring this truth to the surface and dare to accuse some of the adult population of hypocrisy, themselves living without the very morals expected of children, I needed to do more than just feel this reality. It was imperative that I "show," in a visual, tactile, spoken and caring way that we adults need to analyze ourselves. I have accomplished this goal with:

1) The creation and completion of my program, "A Life in Pieces," which includes this book, and also manuals for pre-marriage, post-marriage, pre-natal, families, schools/day-cares, workplaces and client-based businesses dealing with persons afflicted with addictions and depression. It also includes a therapeutic puzzle, designed and built by myself, that lives with the couple, client, student, and/or family members who can then see, feel and be reminded of their great virtues and capabilities as they are inscribed on the pieces of each puzzle.

2) The oral presentation I readied and subsequently deliver for workshops promoting change, acceptance and equality, all leading to genuine peace.

3) Intense observation and research of adult behavior and attitudes, other cultures and religions, and also the effects of abuse on a victim of any age.

4) The recorded successes of "A Life in Pieces."

One of the greatest successes observed in my presentations, and also in the implementation of "A Life in Pieces" was, and will continue to be, a testament to the human spirit. It excites and assures me to witness participants willfully and enthusiastically accept the truth that a popular character trait of many adults is hypocrisy, that many adults are demanding and perhaps void of emotion, making it difficult to appreciate relationships with them. My participants prove that I do not need to be afraid to reveal the need for change. Unoffended and eagerly, these adults accept the suggested paradigm shift promoting harmony, beginning with the fair treatment of our children and the exaltation of their already existing virtues. Surprising to them, they enter my workshop wanting to find ways to change and improve the children/students in their care, then leave realizing it is they who are different; they have been changed.

The force of energy I deliver through my words, and stories of success, have left participants with a sense of enlightenment, hope and joy. The conclusion I believe, is that "A Life in Pieces" solidifies the truth that equal rights for all can be genuinely had, that this is not merely an illusion. The teacher participants who have attended my workshops are not afraid to explore their teaching methods after I explain that the expectations we place on children in regards to virtue training (in other words, social-skill training or child-rearing) are impossible to interpret as black and white, therefore difficult to teach. It becomes clear that social skills, and expectations with regards to each skill, can be misinterpreted, and/or trained with various levels of strictness. In this light, many questions are raised regarding the validity of our modern-day child-rearing techniques. All of this indicates to me that many are humbled by "A Life in Pieces." To me it is a dream that many have waited for, but dared not venture into because it is frightening and argumentative to suggest that we, as a human race, obliterate what we know as our righteous obligations (like training children) and start over again. This willingness to venture into a paradox is to be respected, as it is more common to be offended by new thoughts than to experience a sense of humility and accept that a contrary approach to living is necessary for all of humanity. The fact is that we can eliminate the process of training our children into productive and caring beings because they already are. This is something my participants have accepted with ease, because they have come to realize the possibility of more positive relationships with their students, their own children, even their spouses and workmates. Even though my workshops thus far have concentrated on younger children and the examples of success from my years teaching kindergarten, I am thrilled that attendees understand it is not a program for just one generation, one gender, one race or religion. We discuss the diversity of the process, and practice ideas that can be used with older students, family and workplaces. "A Life in Pieces" is for all persons, for any relationship, and it has all the elements (visual, tactile, oral, and intellectual) necessary to impart the truth that we are all what we need to be; what enlightenment, what a dream.

This book is a very important part of the dream, as it is a powerful way for many to realize this revolutionary solution to peace without being in my presence. It is a way to share my spiritual growth, which has expanded to include passionate child activist. I have concentrated much of my involvement and research on equal rights for children, largely because the devastation and desperation felt when these rights are violated, or non-existent, is world-wide—encompassing children, adults, families, communities and countries. Believing in equality for all children has engaged me in a process of achieving life-altering goals in families, schools, workplaces and communities to improve environments that house children. Improving the environments of adults who have relationships with children is necessary to achieve this goal because, as my life tool has come to clearly demonstrate, we are all closely connected, like an assembled puzzle, where our emotions directly affect one another's. Therefore, trust me as I attempt change through "A Life in Pieces," creating the much needed empathy in adults who are trying to understand, train, and perhaps even change children.

Joy is evident as participants come to trust my conclusion that it transcends explanation to look into the eyes of children who are told they are already kind. I cannot tell you what this does to my heart. Excitement is obvious as I share the success that has been achieved through "A Life in Pieces" in marriages that were once desperate. Calm is felt as I repeatedly express the phrase "exalting the spirit," words that can broaden understanding of divine human nature and lead to a societal change that is so huge I believe any God would rejoice with energy intense enough to shake the earth.

I am empowered by the simple, yet profound truth that the formation of "A Life in Pieces" came about, not because of research that impassioned me to explore reasons for injustice, thus finding a solution to peace, but because my heart and my own experiences did. I sensed and found this solution to peace from the very depths of my being, and it is research and other's shared familiar experiences that consummated my heartfelt knowledge, adding the passion to keep going. The truth is that we do not need research to tell us the world is a better place when we engage in empathetic, fair relationships. Our heart, our innocence, and the powerful emotion of love instill this understanding in us all. The human race declares the need for relationships built on respect and tenderness. Therefore we do not require research to tell us that if we, as adults, do not want to be bossed around, insulted, humiliated, yelled at, spanked, bullied, abused, hit, timed out, condemned and/or raped, then do not do it to a child. Grown-ups, if we do not want to be misinterpreted, an act leading to feelings of defensiveness, insult, confusion, anger, and perhaps frustration and desperation if done often, neither does a child. Grown-ups, if we want, and need, the opportunity to clarify our actions without being told to be quiet, or being labeled oppositional, so do children. Grown-ups, we want just treatment because it makes us happy. If we want to be happy, we must make the children around us happy. It is that simple.

I came to realize that some of the children I have known, who live(d) in abusive and tormenting homes, classrooms and institutions, may never be happy. Many of these children will likely live a life where it is they who will be violent, delinquent, addicted, mentally ill and/or suicidal, unless there is a change in attitude toward them by adults. It is amazing how patience and silence consume my participants as I express insight about the hearts and lives of the children I have taught. The silence eerily continues as I stress how this change of attitude that emphasizes the need to treat children as they themselves want to be treated, and also calming expectations and allowing children to be curious about their life, will change the lives of both child/student and the adult. It is through the sad lives of my students, consisting of such horrors as parental addictions, mental illness, sexual, physical and/or emotional abuse, that I know negative attitudes still exist, and we are failing our young people.

I am delighted to share the paradox that allows the progressive change from failure to success; from control to equality. You are about to read a condensed version of the ideas and thoughts behind the scenes of my program. Condensing this material was a difficult task to complete not only because of the vast feelings and emotions produced by, but also the understanding and successes realized from "A Life in Pieces." In this vastness, I look forward to everyone who comes to relate to its message. I emphasize, and need you to remember, that this is not written to reprimand adults. It is not a generalization stating that all adults are failing, nor is it a generalization that no adults are. I want you to realize I understand and empathize with adults who are abused by other adults, and yes, even by children. I am currently writing the second book of my series, "A Marriage Life in Pieces," to engage this process that will enable better relationships and equality among spouses and family members. "A Life in Pieces: A Piece-by-Piece Guide to Realizing Harmony in Families, Schools and Communities," is my first message of hope. It focuses on children, asking that all adults listen patiently as I help you understand that it comes as such a relief to give up training any child to become what we deem to be a worthy human being. Whether you see yourself, your spouse, co-worker, et cetera, in some of these examples or not, the message in this process will give you an enlightened, fresh experience. By letting go, I have allowed myself to be delighted in the true character of children, and I have come to enjoy, not be annoyed by the eagerness in my own children, their friends and my students— an emotion that often causes them to be jittery and hyper. Instead of silencing their energy and curiosity, thus their personality, I now learn through their genuine emotions and feelings. I relax in calm as I give up commanding and regulating the play of children in my care, where I once watched obsessively and expectedly for inappropriate behaviors, ready to command disciplinary action for the child's own good. I realized that I felt no guilt in my heart if my unfairness caused oppositional behavior in a child, a natural defense mechanism expressing the need for a change in attitude directed toward him/her. Now I do, because I feel I have been hurtful. I no longer try to control children and create little "me's."

I pray I do justice in this message. As you continue on this journey, feeling life through the heart of the world's children, please remember to live in the spirit of the child you were, and continue to be. Feel the emotional succession of your actions in your heart first, then decide if you should proceed to do it to a child. If it is unfair, insulting or presumptuous (to name only a few), please do not carry through because the child will feel the same. I believe it is necessary to bring injustice and inequality to light, because learning how wide and deep abuses are towards children, and realizing the horrific consequences of these abuses, makes for a wiser and more caring individual. This enlightenment produces social, economic, personal and professional growth and it is so easy to live life in such beauty.

My awakening was finding the reasons why, I believe, we continue to fail.

CHAPTER THREE

IGNORANCE AND ASSUMPTION

Two characteristics of mankind that I believe to be responsible for much of the unhappiness in families, schools, communities and societies are ignorance and assumption. "Ignorance," as defined by *Webster's College Dictionary*, means lack of knowledge or learning. "Assume" means to take for granted, or without proof. These are dangerous realities I have examined carefully and felt whole-heartedly in order to understand their potentially catastrophic results. It is ironic that the very word ignorant intrigued me so much that I wanted nothing more than to discover infinite amounts of information regarding why we choose, and allow, it to exist at all.

One of my first discoveries is the fact that ignorance exists due to an individual's interpretation of words, implementing them in every day use without knowing, nor being interested in, their true meaning. This is especially frightening when describing one's first impressions and opinions of a person's character, because first impressions do have an impact on the kind of relationships that ensue. For example, I now cringe at my educated interpretation and knowledge of the word "bad" when I hear it used to describe a child and his/her behavior. I shudder when I think of the negative connotation it casts on this child, an opinion that can/may become permanently attached to his/her psyche. Bad, as defined by *Webster's College Dictionary*, means "failing to reach an acceptable standard; unfavorable; morally objectionable; mischievous; disobedient; disagreeable; unpleasant; and as a very general term, applicable to anyone or anything morally reprehensible." While using these definitions to describe the character of a husband and/or wife, I tried to imagine a relationship of like

15

or love existing between them. I easily concluded from the awareness I now have through word definitions, that the feelings of like or love are highly improbable. Not only would I keep my distance from a disagreeable, morally objectionable husband, but because my attitude towards him would show dislike, he too would want nothing to do with me. I sense a sad end to this relationship, because neither spouse would want to help or learn from the other.

As obvious as the relationship between two adults would be greatly affected if one or both were deemed to possess bad character, it is as obvious in determining the likelihood of a compatible relationship with a child who is defined as such. I feel no positive attachment to any of the meanings of the word "bad," contrary to what I feel when reading definitions of words like "bright" and "beauty," which give me joy and warmth. I have no desire to build a partnership with anyone defined negatively, whether it be an adult or child. Just thinking of being in the presence of an unpleasant person builds anxiety, and I wonder how I can enjoy his/her company. To me, the relationship that develops between an adult and a mischievous, disagreeable child will likely disintegrate with a feeling of dislike that grows as a result of being in the company of someone who is stressful to be around. As this feeling of dislike festers, adult and child become more emotionally distanced, and little affection or positive interaction will occur between the adult and the bad child. It is hard, even impossible, to be happy with and learn from the adult who may then be treating this child as an outcast. Stress and frustration become apparent in such interactions and a nightmare ensues. It is very likely this nightmare started with the (mis)interpretation of a child's character and behaviors as bad because of the ignorance to the meaning of the word. This impression and description of character may live with this child forever. This truth is bad.

Realizing the negative consequences as a result of labeling someone bad, I found it was time to study many harsh words, then challenge myself to think about the right I had to use them when describing a child or adult. This awoke many truths in me, namely the consequence of serious harm to any person when negative words, such as "irritating" and "deviant," are used to describe their personality. I stopped interpreting words like "unpleasant" and "disagreeable" as non-consequential, thinking such character descriptions would not affect a student or me in any negative way. I began challenging myself to use the genuine meaning of all words, trying then to use them only when appropriate. I have almost eliminated any word associated with bad from my vocabulary when describing true character, especially in regards to children; not one child I know suits this label. I came to the conclusion that we misuse and over-use many harmful labels, especially when describing children, and the negative impact to the child and the adult is huge.

Due to the process involved in "A Life in Pieces," I have learned to replace negative words such as "bad," "interrupting" and "disruptive," with positive ones like "warm," "eager" and "cheerful." As learning replaced my ignorance, I found that the antics of an eager and happy child unable to sit still, with hands in lap and a quiet mouth because he/she wants to scream out and jump up and down, are the same as a child labeled as disruptive, hyper and interrupting. Note the difference in the feeling one gets when using the negative terms vs. the positive. There is an immediate change in emotional connections when a child's "name" shifts from irritating, annoying and bad, to eager and excited, with the understanding that these emotions are felt wholeheartedly. Feel this fact as you follow me through an example of the process involved in "A Life in Pieces," then answer the following question: Which would you rather be labeled as: disruptive, morally reprehensible and hyper, or eager, cheerful and happy?

Step One: Write what you believe to be the word definition, then use the dictionary to see how close you were to the true meaning. This is fun to do and will likely show how narrow your understanding was before your word explorations. I was ignorant to every word. You can grow in the meaning by looking up key words from the original. The following are defined by the *Webster's College Dictionary*:

1) **Disruptive**: to throw into disorder; to cause to break down
   disorder- breach of order; public disturbance; to destroy the order or regular arrangement of
2) **Morally reprehensible**: **moral**: of pertaining to or concerned with the principles of right conduct or the distinction between right and wrong; virtuous; upright
   reprehensible- deserving rebuke or censure; blameworthy

rebuke- express sharp, stern disapproval of; reprimand

censure- strong or vehement expression of disapproval; to criticize in a harsh manner

vehement- characterized by rancor or anger

3) **Hyper:** very excitable or nervous; over-excited; keyed up; hyper active; obsessively concerned

4) **Eager:** characterized by keen or enthusiastic desire or interest; impatiently longing; characterized by, or revealing earnestness or expectancy

earnestness or to be earnest in intent- serious in intent, purpose or effort, showing depth or sincerity of feeling

expectancy- the quality or state of expecting; the state of being expected

5) **Cheerful:** full of cheer; in good spirits; pleasant; bright; wholehearted; ungrudging

ungrudging- not begrudging; not reluctant or resentful

6) **Happy:** delighted, pleased or glad; characterized by pleasure, contentment or joy

Step Two: Place the phrase "I am" in front of all the words and repeat the phrases. For example: "I am disruptive and the cause of the break-down; I am reprehensible and deserving of harsh punishment; I am earnest and sincere; I am in good spirits and I am bright."

Step Three: Create the feelings experienced with each of these affirmations through such activities as copying the word down, concentrating on each individual letter (feel the word); writing a song or poem; and/or drawing a picture. Allow yourself to express opposition to a word, if necessary, through feelings of insult and humiliation. Allow your heart to smile with words that bring joy, calm and contentment. Explore the function and usability of each word and decide if you have been ignorant of its true meaning.

Step Four: Answer the question: What would I rather be "named": disruptive, morally reprehensible and hyper, or eager, cheerful and happy?

My earnest answer is that I sincerely want to be called eager, cheerful and happy because this is how I feel. If I seem hyper in another's opinion, it is because I am loving life. I wholeheartedly do not want to be called disruptive and morally reprehensible because they are untrue and harsh, and will affect any relationship I am in. I have come to realize that because of the huge difference in meaning, and therefore in response to these contrary labels, I know everyone else will choose the same. I must always relate to children through positive descriptions, this being a life changing conclusion, as children generally are not allowed to object to adverse character descriptions. This inability to scream out injustice causes so much pain. Using words that we, as adults, would gladly accept, and eliminating ones that are offensive, is the beginning of the journey to peace. This is not a new revelation, but it is one that is often forgotten.

Another one of my discoveries involving ignorance and assumption is mankind's ability to ignore (not use) the infinite resource of words when in relationships with others. Think about this. In the absence of words to describe character, such as helpful, bright, and beautiful, it is easy to implement the word bad. A heart devoid of the meaning, or use, of words describing excellence can easily be penetrated and overtaken with words describing behaviors assumed to be annoying, deviant, noncompliant, et cetera. Rarely, if ever, are the adjectives "kind" and "bad" used in the same sentence or felt at the same time in your heart. How can one overthrow the negative and empower the positive, allowing the brain to intensify the good? By learning about, then repeating anytime and anyplace, the words of excellence. Imagine a situation with your own children or spouse/partner when an "inappropriate" act is taking place, causing a surge of annoyance and build-up in anger. This can lead to a rush of negative adrenaline, not one of the rushes that are exhilarating with excitement and fun or used to save a pet from a fire, but one causing lack of thinking and impulsivity. At this moment there are basically two choices: the first is using the word knowledge that you have gained to recognize that your child or spouse is kind and warm, therefore not intentionally irritating or mean. It is then easy to let go of the frustration that could build, allowing calm to take hold, assuring you this was really no big deal. This is the scenario that builds with the process of "A Life in Pieces" because words of virtue have been investigated and shared through masterpieces of song, art and poetry, and are now felt whole-heartedly within the recesses of the mind and heart. Words like benevolence, human affection and intimacy will be remembered by inscribing them on your life puzzle that can be displayed for all to see. There is no insult or anger. The second choice, one that has ignored the use and meaning of positive words, has no emotional substitute for the probable anger that has begun and likely will intensify. This can build a rush of adrenaline and frustration, helping to cement in your mind and heart that the person before you is bad and frustrating. This thought will fester, actually causing the next moment of frustration, and the next to become more impulsive and emotionally draining. The more experiences one has that cause the release of adrenaline, the more agitated and stressed one becomes. The more impulsive and stressed one becomes, creating increased anger, the less likely the body will be able to find the calm that will enable a person to redirect feelings and connect with words of kindness. As a result, positive affirmations will likely not be used in context with negative affirmations like, "bad" and "reprehensible." Therefore, when calling an adult and/or child bad, this very likely means one is devoid of the very language (warm, happy, affectionate, fortunate) that could switch that label to beautiful.

A perfect example of this fact is the relationship that developed between myself and one of my young students who, during the start of our kindergarten year together, was placed in a three-week behavioral observation program with overnight stays away from home and in-facility schooling. Upon her return to our program, she was on medication due to oppositional behavior (kicking and swearing) and defiance. Immediately, my heart empathized with this young child, which was something very important at this time, yet something I found lacking in the heart of others. At no time did I hear the obvious fact that she was traumatized (a good word for this situation that was ignored) and scared when, at five years old, she was whisked away from her home and her family to be in the presence of strangers who watched her every move, taught her, fed her and put her to bed every night. She was disagreeing with this situation that she had no say in, showing every adult involved in this step to make her a "better" person that it is difficult for anyone to behave when confused and filled with fear. The expectations placed upon her were too much for this little girl. She was opposing her removal from her family and her home, and was showing her discontent in any way that she could. It was not hard to see that her behavior problems were a direct result of trauma, thus causing her to be difficult (a word they used without trepidation). I came to this realization very simply by asking myself what I would do if I were her, even at my age. I have no doubt that being removed from my home and family, and placed in the care of strangers, would make me angry, unhappy, helpless and afraid, resulting in a change in my behavior for the worse. Yet, I would have known in my heart I was not bad; there would be no need to medicate me, I would just want to go home.

This simple truth allowed me to interact in a way that was a complete contrast to that of the program professionals she encountered throughout her ordeal. This was because I chose not to ignore the girl's feelings and went even further by comparing my feelings with that of this child in the same situation. I found it impossible to think she could have reacted any differently. I also paid attention to the words that were used to describe her behavior resulting in the negative label and the need for medication. I found the words reprehensible and refused to use them.

Because of these steps, I began working with her the way I would have appreciated help from someone after a traumatic experience. I sought to immediately intensify her innate beauty (that I had now investigated) and told her she is all she needs to be: "You are kind. You warm my heart. You make me comfortable, and you help me so much." In no time she calmed her emotions and felt safe with me, finding comfort in my words and eventually started repeating them. As I intensified her beauty with more words from the investigated meanings, along with the help of our classroom puzzle to prove to her she is connected by goodness, it was decided from home that she be taken off medication. The year spent with this child became one of the defining moments for "A Life in Pieces." This little student excelled in proving her innate virtues and, as her mother stated, was no longer a problem at home. This little beauty was a gift to the class, using the classroom words and puzzle to describe her fellow classmates, and redirect their behavior. Her favorite word was beauty, which became the word she started every pretend classroom time with. She shared joy with the other students using "eager," "bright," and many more words that will be defined in chapter eleven. Her improved learning and social interconnectedness were very evident.

The words of virtue could no longer be ignored by her, or any of our four to six year-olds, because we examined, analyzed and intensified them together. Only joy was felt at graduation as the spirit of all the students was deepened in the speech to the class. There was hope that the excellence in all the children would continue to be strengthened the next year and in the following years. Sadly and tragically, negative affirmations must have greatly exceeded positive because my little angelic student was expelled before the end of grade one. This was an unacceptable conclusion a few short months after her attendance in my class. This disturbing end would have been less probable with the implementation and use of "A Life in Pieces," where words are never ignored, nor are they taken for granted.

Ignoring the use of positive affirmations while ignorantly using negative labels is a way to eliminate any responsibility in the underachievements of others. If a disobedient child/student fails in school or is expelled it may be concluded that this was the consequence of her being morally objectionable, unfavorable, disobedient—you get the picture. It has nothing to do with the adults in her life. Or does it? When I started to pay attention to, and intensify, the excellence in every child in my care, I instantaneously paid attention to the kind of atmosphere I provided them for success because I knew they were ready to succeed in every way. I shifted the paradigm (changed traditional thoughts and patterns) when I began to look at myself (the adult), and my unjust behavior toward the students when they were misbehaving. I realized that, because they exude kindness and grace, they would not intentionally harm or disrespect me, nor would they intentionally interfere with the happiness or progress in their relationships and learning. Therefore, I am beginning to realize that grown-ups are responsible for much of the frustration in children, thus causing disruptive behaviors. Adults can be responsible for their failures due to the negative emotional impact that obvious feelings, such as dislike, have on the intellectual and social abilities of a child. As adults change their negative behavior toward children, creating more positive and calmer relationships, children can be happier and more productive, thus less anxious, frustrated and angry. This fact has led me to many proud moments as I have realized, through the implementation of "A Life in Pieces," that I have imbued the heart of these children/students with calm, safety, respect, and more positive feelings. This is a fact that would have contributed to a very proud moment for the teacher(s) of my previous student and would have kept this little beauty in class, her spirit alive and intact. But unfortunately, because obviously little or no attention was paid to the excellence of this child, there was likely no sadness felt by the teacher(s) over the actions she took in expelling this six-year-old child. I hold onto my changed world where all words are important; where I no longer ignore any combination of letters that symbolize life. For this reason I am overjoyed that I can be different and happy, yet at the same time disturbed, sad, and frustrated that adults can get away with so much with little or no consequences for their actions. I believe the word "unfair" is applicable here.

The discoveries continued with the awareness of the dangerous practice of assuming that all we hear and read is the truth and makes sense. We assume that we do not need to read or think things through to understand if what is being said or done is productive and correct. Perhaps this is because of habit, time constraints, or the belief that we already know everything anyway. Because of these assumptions, combined with the fact that the skills of perception and insight (the feeling that something is wrong) are rarely used, relationships and programs are often left in a dysfunctional state. It is this realization that changed and intensified my life. Because of the negative consequences related to the practice of assuming all is correct, I delved into intense thinking and feeling and discovered there are a large number of programs that instigate a negative change, actually making things worse instead of better. I have come to understand why it is easier to be ignorant to what occurs around us. Leaving ignorance behind can be a disheartening, difficult awakening, one in which courage is required.

It is frightening to realize the multitude of people who believe ignorance is okay, especially in struggling relationships. When we do not engage the hidden talents that stimulate our senses, such as perception and empathy, adults often repeat the same techniques that claim to improve, for example a misbehaving child, even if these techniques have failed, and continue to fail in providing positive change. It does not make sense to keep trying programs that fail to calm nerves due to increased distress felt by all persons. When positive change does not happen, there should be attempts to change an entire approach and research (with the aid of our senses) a more approving one.

Many grown-ups and child-oriented program facilitators think it makes sense, for example, to continue to implement the over-used (my belief) time-out approach for a child sitting improperly through a movie, dinner, class, et cetera, without finding out why this behavior is occurring. With this technique, it is unlikely that much, or any investigation of the negative consequences resulting from the use of aversion therapy for "disrespectful" children has taken place. In the above example, it may be believed that removal from the situation to punish the child is the solution to what the adult labels as intolerant behavior without realizing the consequences of his/her actions on the child, or him/herself, when doing so. This creates a barrier that will likely affect the relationship between them, especially if similar situations often present themselves. Because little effort will likely be invested in discovering why the child is having a difficult time sitting, therefore eliminating any chance of discovering new and appropriate solutions, the likelihood of increased anxiety will be high. This reality makes it more difficult for the child to pay attention and sit, thus causing more anxiety, leading sometimes to desperation. Then it is time for stress leave! How do you like the cycle? This is the cause for very stressful relationships between a teacher and student, a child and parent(s), and even the parents themselves.

What does make sense is to ignite the thinking center of the brain, instructing it to learn some of the possible reasons as to why this child may be overreacting. Better yet, with "A Life in Pieces," you will immediately understand the respectful nature of your child/student who is kind and warm, allowing you to think of a logical reason for the disruption. Young children especially do not act out to make you angry or gain revenge, so it is likely that they are excited, or bored, or perhaps sick, or even sad—but not bad. It is very calming to investigate what emotions lead to certain types of behaviors, and what behaviors exude certain virtues. They can then be dealt with properly.

Imagine this: A young girl arrives home after an awesome day at school. She is hyper and full of energy because she cannot wait to tell her parents about the surprise birthday party she was given at school that afternoon. She had not expected this and the surprise was the best ever. The excitement from the afternoon carried over to home time. At home, as her parents were preparing dinner, she attempted to explain her joy. In the rush, her parents asked that she remain silent. She became more anxious and excited, making it impossible to sit still or stay quiet because her tummy was tickling with earnestness as the need to share her story intensified. Because of the urgency of her behavior, her parents could take no more, telling her she was disrespectful and demanded she be quiet and go to her room. She remained silent until morning and never did share her story. The sadness felt when her joy was ignored, joined with the humiliation and frustration felt when reprimanded for having something exciting to share, quieted this little girl for a very long time. This was not the first time she was timed-out for wanting to share her life.

This did not make sense. All she wanted was to be respected for being a child; eager to share and feel cheerful, exuberant, earnest and happy. It would have taken a few joyous moments to share her story, but even less time for the parent to have investigated the reason for her behavior, thus coming to a successful conclusion, even if it was to affirm that the child could share her story at a better time. Find reasons, discover answers. Give respect, get respect. The act of not learning, then assuming this makes sense, does not make sense.

Imagine this true story of a young child I know: A five-year-old girl, the victim of Fetal Alcohol Spectrum Disorder (FASD), was aggravating and irritating the teachers in her first grade class. This young girl was often timed out at the X spot on the wall for, what the teachers defined as, not listening in class. Without investigating possible reasons for her misbehavior, it was assumed she was being intentionally bad when interrupting, a thought that allowed the teachers to continue labeling this little student using such descriptive words as "disobedient" and "disrespectful." It became evident to the little girl, her mother, and myself that she was disliked by the teachers when negative messages indicating she was bad, were written almost daily in her agenda. I was frustrated and confused with this interpretation because I knew this child and she is one who exudes cheerfulness, obedience, and beauty. My frustration grew with the implementation of time-out for punishment, with the teachers assuming this method was a positive approach to eliminating the interpreted bad behaviors. I questioned the appropriateness of the aversion techniques. I understand that not knowing about traumas in a child's life may be an excuse for an adult to use inappropriate techniques, including yelling at the child. Adults use excuses like "they did not know," or "if only they had known": "If only I had known she was sexually abused the night before, I would have been kinder and gentler." In this case, assumptions and claiming ignorance were definitely not appropriate.

This little girl's past was disclosed by the mother, and this disclosure indicated to the teachers (if they cared to listen and empathize) very likely reasons for the disruptive behavior. Prior to the enrollment at this new school, a meeting was held with one of the teachers, the mom, and myself, to disclose that this child, from the age of three, was sexually abused by her brother. At the time of the meeting it was not known this abuse was still occurring. Because of the disclosure, it was hoped that empathy and compassion would be found in this very difficult, stressful time. Research has disclosed for years that any kind of abuse towards children will cause a change in behavior, making the tasks of listening, sitting, and even learning more difficult. These truths give teachers and parents the opportunity to adjust to abused, vulnerable children, allowing more love and compassion to be included in their everyday activities and chores. Everyone learns better with love. In this case, the abused child had to adjust to the expectations of the adult. The disclosure of sexual abuse was obviously ignored, taken for granted, assumed to be nothing of consequence to this young girl. No effort was taken to assure that school would not add to her trauma. The blatant continual, inexcusable ignorance and increased time-outs escalated the anxiety of going to school, and the behavior continued to be punished. At a time when she screamed out for help, needing someone to hear her pain, she was cast aside at the X, continually judged by the teachers. She is now attending a different school and I have introduced her to her "life in pieces," calming her as she acknowledges that she is not a bad girl; she is all God wants her to be. Thank goodness she survived a time when she needed help. Thank goodness she got help; not all children do.

Now, aware of the need to rid this world of ignorance and assumptions, imagine a child's cry:

A Child's Cry

When I was born, I was:
Wanting and needing your love, that is what God teaches,
I trusted you to help in my life as we met new parents, friends and teachers.

I was innocent in assuming you would be like the parent next door,
But something happened along the way, my dreams turned to night-
mares when you threw me to the floor.

My spontaneity made you mad; you never wanted to play,
I waited patiently without anger or complaint, just to tell you the
good things the teacher had to say.

You never did care to hear me talk, or join in my fun.
You never cared that I was loving and kind; oh God, I did not know
I was picked to be the "one."

To lose my humble, meek self, as I lost trust in those who never let
me "be,"
Who yelled at and beat me, and when in bed it was my body he wanted to see.

To anyone who will hear, I am sorry you know me so tough,
But life for me got really rough.

Please, I am trying to say, when I hit, kick and shove,
Help me find me again, the one who just wanted love.

Please, will you help?

Eliminating ignorance has cast a defining light on how I now live and
view the world. I will never again define any child as being out of
control, vengeful, spiteful, deviant, or delinquent. Instead, I will see
a tormented child, with a soul screaming for understanding and love.
There will be no X on the wall.

Because of my previous ignorance and assumptions, I have come
to redefine everything about life.

CHAPTER FOUR

REDEFINING LIFE

This part of the journey begins with three questions I often ask myself:

1) Why did I assume it is, and always has been, necessary for adults to teach morals and values to children?
2) Why did I assume adults are capable of the impossible task of teaching these?
3) Why did I assume children are incapable of growing in harmonious relationships without adult intervention?

I am amused as I imagine myself as an all-knowing grown-up who has, of course, passed through the gates of moral baptism. I am conversing with other morally baptized grown-ups about the problems we assume children inherit, such as lack of concern regarding the decencies of their behavior and their lack of ability to distinguish between right and wrong. At this point, I am taking into consideration the fact that if virtue and excellence have to be taught, then virtue and excellence are lacking at the present time. This allows me to conclude that if excellence is not reared into our children they will become emotionally illiterate hooligans and the world will be ruled by human bodies with no heart and soul. I share this in conversation:

> "Children do not know how to behave. They lack the skills needed for friendship, compassion, and co-operation. They are not respectful or empathetic, therefore will not care about the consequences of their

actions or the feelings of others. Children are selfish, manipulative, and unreasonable. Children bully each other and are aggressive. No wonder the world has so many problems. Thank goodness we adults know how to change this."

I imagine myself saying these words and I am sad, realizing my tone of self-righteousness and arrogance. I am disheartened, hearing the dislike for, and misunderstanding of, children that is expressed by these words. I am confused. Do I think I am perfect enough to teach what is most critical in life? Do I think thoughts, such as the above, will not affect my feelings toward and opinions of children? What is written above may sound a little extreme, but I guarantee that after years of experience with children personally, voluntarily, and professionally, I know this thinking is not unusual or over-blown. I have heard and read the same or similar words voiced by many adults who describe children in this way. They obviously do not feel sad or controlling, nor do they express an urgency to redefine their perception of our youngest, most vulnerable beings in the world.

I am proud to say my day for redemption has come and it is time to reorganize my thoughts, rid my brain of my ignorance and arrogance, and redefine my interpretation of the role and capabilities of children, adults, and myself. So, with eagerness and joy I investigate and redefine child-rearing ideals implemented not only in the home, but also in schools, daycares, churches—basically any environment that shares the idea that children have to be trained into moral and righteous adults.

Some school advertisements welcome students who, they say, will learn to lead full and productive lives because they will be taught the necessary morals and values needed to do so in the school. In my days of ignorance, I paid no attention to the words that made up this statement and I carried on, arrogantly thinking that I would/could contribute to the instillation of morals in my students through teaching an infinite number of necessary social skills, like remembering the rules and remembering the consequences of one's actions (even for two to five-year-old children). In my enlightenment, I shudder at the real message behind the words "will learn," because this implies absence of the skill to be taught. There then has to be, or should be, someone qualified enough to teach it. But is there? To be qualified to teach a skill and expect its perfection, the teacher/parent will have had to pass it him/herself. Since questioning the validity of this advertisement that seems to profile the adult as all-knowing and righteous, I shudder at the real expectations of these social skills that I believe are impossible even for adults to fulfill. I think of grown-ups following all the rules, like being kind and respectful to one another. This statement of expectation screams of hypocrisy. Any media updating the progress of peace in families, communities and countries, such as newspapers and magazines, proves that this rule is often not followed. I imagine adults complying and succeeding with the expected rule to remember the consequences of their actions and see, and accept, failure in order to instigate change and improve relationships. If the consequences of our actions leading to racism, divorce, addictions, abuse, depression, war, et cetera were remembered, it is clear we would be living in a different world, while gaining some progress in ensuring equality and tranquility for all. But, we are not. Why do we continue to fail?

I believe failure occurs for a number of reasons, three being the assumptions mentioned at the beginning of this chapter. Repeatedly, adults who are not perfect are responsible for teaching perfection. This sets the stage for impossible expectations on children, even the adults, affecting one's present and future. Adults ignorantly, gladly, or perhaps unwillingly, assume the impossible role of teaching morals to children whom they feel are void of what they deem valuable and productive traits. Why else would they have to be taught? I have turned my ignorance into inquisition and I ask a few questions:

1. Why do some grown-ups not question the validity of this ignorance?
2. Why is it assumed that children can master humanitarian goals when many adults cannot?
3. Why is it assumed that these can actually be taught?
4. Why is it not accepted, with joy, that all persons inherit innate goodness at conception, readying them with the desire and knowledge to ignite the world with kindness and grace?
5. Have we grown-ups been led in the wrong direction, misinterpreting our roles as peace-builders, and our success in achieving moral perfection ourselves?

6. Why have we, as a society, not found the urgency to look deep into the negative, habitual thoughts and actions practiced by the adult population in order to turn failure into success?

My conclusions are these. Firstly, because it is not common practice for adults to pay attention to or remember the consequences of their actions, supposedly a necessary prerequisite for any social skill. Secondly, because assuming adult responsibility regarding any displeasure, disharmony, or disrespect is insulting and unheard of. It is easier placing blame on the shoulders of children who "do not know how to behave" and cannot fight back. Thirdly, because ironically, in order to succeed and find a world where humanity thrives, it must be recognized that it is not the children who need moral education, it is the grown-ups. I know these are allegations and interpretations that will cause unrest in some people, but fortunately to myself and many others, it is by recognizing these truths that turn potential failures into success stories. Continue to reevaluate and redefine with me to solidify the fact that you, too, can find success.

I began to see life differently when I reorganized my thoughts, creating in me the need to redefine the school advertisement to allow a better understanding of what is being sold:

> "Parents, send your children to our school. We welcome your "unproductive" child who does not yet know, or use, the necessary skills that allow him/her to co-exist respectfully with others. You will be pleased as the adults in our school begin moral instruction when your children are very young and will continue until their final year. We feel confident in our approach and our understanding of these skills that we have, of course, successfully accomplished. We follow each social skill and rule expected of our students, so we are permitted to ask the same of them. We will not allow hypocrisy."

I am uncomfortable (as I am sure many are, but cannot say) with what I think is a better, clearer understanding of the message sent out by some of our schools. I am fearful of such a general statement, like "will learn the necessary morals and values to become productive people," because life values cannot be interpreted in one way by all. Think about this important fact: an adult's idea of what is moral, productive, valuable, and excellent is based on religion, culture, gender, age, living conditions, past and present relationships, patience, whether they are sick, hot, stressed, and so on. Therefore, the idea of finding a black and white definition and description of each social skill and moral virtue is impossible, because the answer is not black and white and can change day-to-day. An example of this fact involves the social skills which expect that three to five-year-olds think before they act and also think of the correct way to act. These, along with all the other skills I have investigated, are very personal in interpretation and expectation. As I make sense of these two skills, I can think of few, if any, scenarios involving young children when it comes to the need to think before acting and the need to think of the correct way to act. Young children have the innate ability to be kind, so they will not intentionally hurt anyone and they are not yet into inappropriate activities such as drugs, vandalism, theft, stabbing, abuse and/or laziness. These are examples of activities where thinking before acting out is a safe course of action. In the case of two to five-year-old children and what could constitute "inappropriate" behaviors that should be thought through before acting upon, I imagine examples such as: the inability to sit quietly, interrupting the class with screams of joy because of expectation and excitement; rambunctious behavior because of the nature of children, and/or the patience, thus encouragement of some culture's acceptance of rowdy children; hyperactivity because of abuse suffered at home; distractibility due to anxiety and fear brought on by bullying at school (by a schoolmate or teacher); crying (many adults dislike children who cry) because of the break-down of a family; and impulsivity due to a rape the night before. All these examples of observable "dislikable" behaviors can be (mis)interpreted and labeled by an adult as incorrect, non-thinking, immoral, and/or disrespectful, thus resulting in the failure of the student to implement the social skill requiring that they think of the correct way to act: quiet, mouth closed, hands in lap, feet under the desk, looking at the teacher.

Without investigating the reasons as to why these behaviors may be occurring, for example an abusive home environment, or the child's natural curiosity, the obvious interrupting, non-attentive behavior will likely lead the adult to conclude that because the disobedient child is not thinking before acting out, he/she must be punished in order to stop the disruption of the class and to decrease the inappropriate behaviors. I find here the presence of ignorance, resulting in a lack of thinking in regards to the fact that the children will be excited again because they are curious about everything. Attention is not paid to the fact that mom and dad may not get back together, so the resulting crying and anxiety will not soon go away. There will also be continued or increased agitation and interruption by a child victim of abuse due to the intense fear and desperation that builds if the abuse does not stop. Therefore there will be a repeat of the behaviors the adults are labeling as bad, causing frustration as each adult attempts to deal with them.

As I came to understand the importance of piecing together the lives of all persons (discovering their "Life in Pieces"), I began to examine and redefine bad behaviors to ensure that I stop and think before disciplining a child. Can a child be truly deviant and selfish? Is a child really oppositional? If he/she is, is this "behavior" legitimate? Is it appropriate that I discipline a child by the way I interpret the intent of his/her behavior? Through "A Life in Pieces," inscribing the meanings of the "bad" words in my brain, then proceeding to inscribe the opposite onto the thirteen puzzle pieces in our class, I came to realize the great number of obstacles interfering with the interpretation of moral expectations. I also came to realize the number of negative obstacles interfering with a child's ability to comply to, and remember rules. I discovered many reasons why discipline is often misused and mismanaged. I engaged myself in the process of finding a solution that would eliminate the obstacles, not increase them. The first step was the positive shift in thinking from the belief that children need to be trained to think before they act in order to act properly, to accepting that they will, to the best of their ability.

Follow a basic day in my classroom implementing the words investigated in "A Life in Pieces." One student, then five students, soon all the students arrive in the morning and are displaying what would be thought of as inappropriate behaviors, including restlessness, loud chatter and non-routine activities. In my not-so-distant past, I would have interpreted the students' behavior as being non-thinking and disrespectful because I assumed they knew the class rules, therefore they should not engage themselves in such uncontrolled behavior or at least change the misbehavior upon command. I now know differently. At the beginning of this school day I am tired from the night before and would prefer that the children find calm, enabling them to follow through with my instructions and learn easily. The best way to ensure this is to first acknowledge to myself that I do not know the reason why the students have come in "out-of-control." Because of this, I will not assume they are misbehaving or intentionally irritating me. I will not isolate one, or a couple, of the children from the group, stating that they are the most misbehaved. Instead I will do the simplest, quickest, most relaxing exchange with all the students to calm them down. I pay attention to the fact that they are eager (this also means being sensitive to something that has occurred, such as abuse of any kind) and happy (meaning they are wanting to jump up and down, talk, laugh and so much more). This simple recognition solidifies in the children that I have an understanding of their feelings and behavior, and they feel respected. This also helps me begin to calm down, because I am happy and proud to be providing an atmosphere that is so pleasing to the students that they outwardly display their contentment and happiness. Furthermore, this gives me the desire to spend a few minutes enjoying their smiles and laughter before it comes time to redirect their behavior, indicating it is time to learn. To bring quiet to the class, I have found success by implementing many words that affirm the ability of the students to calm down and listen. There is an improvement in learning and memory when anyone's day starts with phrases like:

> "Students, you are eager and excited today. We know what those words mean because we have talked about them. We all know what it feels like to be excited. You have tummies that are tickling and making your whole body move. You feel like you might explode! I know this is difficult when you are at school and have to pay attention, but I also know you are kind and caring, thinking of me in your heart. I know you are patient, meaning you can calm the ticklies down and

not be mad when you are asked to do so. You bright children, I know you understand what I am saying, so let us get started."

or

"You bright students (husband, employees, friends), you look so happy today. You are making me smile already. We are going to have a very productive day. I know we can start our lesson now, and you children can listen and learn very well. I am thinking about you, and I want to be the best teacher today. I want to do a great job, so I need you to find your patience."

Success is realized because these students learn so much better, remember so much more, and are socially accepting of all in the class when I intensify and remind them of their capability to respect and cooperate. The students respect not because they have to, but because they want to.

If the hyperactivity, for whatever reason, does not stop and there seems a need to discipline, I have created a discipline approach that is easy to relate to. It keeps the spirit intact and lets the children know they are still cared for. For example, instead of accusing an excited child of disrupting the class, being irritating or annoying, and then punishing this behavior, I pay attention to the fact that this child may be excited, expressing the need to communicate something that has created a sense of eagerness felt throughout his/her entire body. I steer the child away from the immediacy of the emotion by explaining that because he/she is patient (the word having now been defined and inscribed on the life puzzle), calm will come with the acceptance that there is a better time to share. I am respecting the fact that this child has the right to feel emotions because I do not make the hyperactivity a negative behavior. I am taking time to pay attention to the emotions felt, showing the student I understand. It may take a few brief moments to calm him/her down, but these few moments are worth the many moments of intensified learning, increased memory and improved social interactions.

Tragically, many adults do not like the rambunctious nature of happy, excited children—especially when they themselves may be tired, sick and/or unhappy. Equally as tragic, many adults do not empathize, or pay attention to the abuses suffered by many children, thus disregarding these as reasons for misbehavior. It is inexcusable that many adults do not know, nor want to know, the traditions of other religions or cultures, therefore they expect behavior that is individual to their beliefs. In these cases, it is the adult who is not thinking before acting and not thinking of the correct way to act, and frustration increases, interfering with the very skills we want children to master: listening, learning, and getting along. Adults often engage in teaching beliefs that are very individual and personal. What one teacher and/or parent expects in fairness and importance, another may be more demanding, or more relaxed with the same expectation. Ignorance is evident in the belief that values can be taught correctly to the masses, or that they can even be taught at all. On the other hand, enlightenment and calm come to all persons who know they already exist.

This realization has changed everything about me. As a young mother and teacher, I reprimanded children/students for "inappropriate" behaviors by engaging in aversive conditioning for punishment, like time out, removal from a fun activity, et cetera. As I harped on a student, especially one who often behaved inappropriately, I became more stressed and unhappy, leading me to dislike this certain child due the constant need to watch and reprimand. As time went on, a vicious cycle began. I was initially calmed, believing that my interpretation of a student's act was right and also that every child could learn to accept the consequences I gave for their bad behavior with no opposition. I believed that after a few punishing consequences the child would understand how to behave properly, as the more the child was exposed to negative stimuli, the more they would dislike it, and the less they would engage in the negative acts. But instead of remaining calm, I became more agitated and lost my temper often, as the behavior did not change with the first request to stop, nor the second, nor even the third. Numerous time-outs and problem solving sessions occurred and it seemed as though things got worse. This continued because I lacked a better way of engaging with the students and, by this time, there was a constant feeling of aggravation. Thankfully I realized that my student(s) and I were getting upset because of me. I often intervened in play and work times because I did not like what the students were doing. This upset both myself and them. I began to calm down once I realized it was time to look at myself and how unfair it was to interpret and judge the students with little knowledge to go on. I began to accept, not be insulted by, the fact that much of the frustration existed because my interpretation of the children's bad, inappropriate behavior was incorrect. This had caused helplessness and confusion in them, especially when I disallowed opposition to my discipline, or my negative behavior. It was time to discipline myself. I needed to realize my errors and the consequences of these on the children so I would not keep repeating the same mistakes.

Obsessing over the necessity to accept wrongful doing, accepting consequences with no opposition, and remembering the consequences so that the behavior is not repeated, is what adults expect of children, not themselves. Therefore this social skill should go under the title of injustice, in the fact that I was allowed to behave how I wanted to towards the children/students, paying little or no attention to the consequences that followed. Children did not get to express their opinions about my actions and behaviors, and if they did, I could label them as oppositional and defiant. Imagine if your partner or spouse did something unfair and you were not allowed to reply or react. It is so unfair to expect anyone to remain silent when they know their rights are being violated, and it is unfathomable to assume that injustice be greeted with a smile and silence by a victim, while at the same time go unnoticed by an abuser.

When whole generations of children are ruled and controlled by grown-ups, permitting many moments of injustice, failure becomes a fact of life. The greatest moment of enlightenment comes with the realization that if I want to see proper behavior and be respected, I have to eliminate any form of injustice towards others. This is the irony of life. In an adult's mind, it is his/her child-rearing ideologies and practices he/she implements that enable the growth of an unproductive child into a productive and compassionate human being. But in truth, it is the adults' thinking that they can succeed in implementing personal values that causes injustice to prevail, therefore the likelihood of successfully producing the adults' version of a productive individual becomes less likely, if not impossible.

My enlightenment was realizing it is inappropriate to believe that adults, or anyone, can teach virtues, because they are impossible to teach. Virtue already exists. The greatest irony of all is that in our attempt to teach moral excellence, we take it away.

CHAPTER FIVE

IRONY

The meaning of irony is very suitable to my new life and the implementation of "A Life in Pieces," because I have realized truths that are contrary to what is expected and believed by much of mankind. I know that to some, these findings will be inappropriate and out of place due to the fact that they are inconsistent with popular belief. The greatest irony of my life revolves around the discovery that respect, joy, and love enrich any relationship when they are assumed to exist already (this is one assumption I indulge in) and are intensified through communication and creation. Harmonious relationships are difficult to attain when virtues are expected, sought out, and then taught (lectured) when it is assumed they are missing. What many adults believe themselves, and indoctrinate in children, is that success is realized through the training of morals and virtues by one righteous, knowing individual (who I believe has a false sense of modesty), to another, whose morals are non-existent.

On a personal note, with this philosophy in mind I attempted to institute change in my marriage (that needed a desperate new beginning) by trying to educate my husband in what is "expected" of human beings: the need to respect the decencies of behavior, think before you act, make sure you act in a kind and respectful manner, et cetera (this is like an expectation from adult to child). I often felt, and expressed, dissatisfaction in his emptiness, and also his inability to see the consequences of his actions. I tried to train him into being a kinder, more compassionate partner (I believed then, that he was acting like a child). Thinking I was capable of such a task and assuming he understood words like respectful and compassionate, I set out on a mission to bring harmony to our lives by reminding him to be kind and empathetic. If this was not of any concern to him, we would have the "talk" about our relationship. This created a more defiant being who felt controlled and always wrong, thus eliminating any chance we had of realizing success. The results of engaging in popular approaches requiring the obsession over problems and the endless debate of stress-provoking issues to improve relationships, were contrary to what I had been told and/or expected. Ironically, instead of realizing positive change, discussion felt like nagging, causing anxiety to build because my husband got tired of the "nagging." Frustration built because I got tired of him not understanding the point I was trying to make, leading to more attempts to get the point across. Homework, or problem solving, used to improve the relationship was never satisfying or pleasing because it was mainly based on what had to be done to eliminate a problem. Issues of dissent that were brought up were immediately fought over, not discussed. Does this sound familiar? Because of these personal experiences I had in attempting to change a tormenting and traumatic existence, I now conclude that these modern-day approaches to harmonizing relationships of any kind are very inappropriate, and rarely succeed in calming the persons involved. It is the obsession and constant "working out the problems" that actually cements their existence. I started to question the process to peace, and hence educated myself in order to change.

How can someone learn virtues when they do not understand what they mean? Is the meaning clear to the person teaching the virtues? My husband did not know what I meant by the words used to express my discontent, and ironically, neither did I. The more I attempted to train my husband to be kind, respectful and caring—instead of rude, unconcerned and angry—the more confused and frustrated we both became. When I realized the flaws were in my belief that the relationship could be changed by concentrating on the failures in order to make them better, I could then redefine my understanding of relationships and success. I realized that if the morals I was attempting to teach were, instead of failing to exist, expressed as already existing, we as a couple would begin the road to recovery. Instead of the expectation to be kind instead of angry, I lived daily with my new truth that kindness was ready and waiting to co-exist with many other virtuous qualities. I had developed a program of success in the midst of despair. At first I could not imagine creating words to intensify the spirit of the one causing me so much pain. I felt it inappropriate displaying words of virtue when I did not think they existed. I did not want to build a false sense of goodness in the one who was displaying no goodness at all. This is, I have come to realize, the same attitude of adults towards some children. This led to increased anxiety, but we both wanted a life together and we were both trying to find solutions. Peace was not close and time was running out, so change was imperative. It was time to assume that kindness and compassion were alive, and begin the paradigm shift. Phrases such as, "That was not kind or respectful, you ruined my day," became, "You are kind, so I know we will have a great day together." It was time to implement our "Life in Pieces," and we began connecting thirteen life pieces of our puzzle instead of watching them come apart.

I want to welcome you to a week in our life, enveloping a process that can lead anyone to a tranquil, fulfilling relationship. "A Life in Pieces," solidified through the inscription of word meanings on our marriage/family life puzzle, has brought calm for a number of reasons. One of the most important is the fact that we understand neither of us is grander than the other and/or always right. This results in a calmer home environment because there is no accusation of nagging or the feeling of always being wrong. Another important change is that energy is no longer consumed on issues of despair. This is because we have gotten into the habit of intensifying virtues through repeated oral expressions relating to the definitions of words like sympathy, courage and humanity. For more reasons than I can mention, we have gratefully come to understand that years of attempting to reduce sorrow with communication about our problems brought anxiety, frustration, desperation and feelings of hate. I introduce you now to my family whose members are all that is beauty.

My virtue creation one particular week was built on beauty. I wanted my family to envision what has grown and blossomed in all of us, so I created a tree with branches defining this virtue. On the first day I pinned the phrase, "my family is beauty" on a branch and placed it on the table for all to see and remember. Each day I added a new meaning of this intense word, and asked my family to read, feel, and remember each new meaning. Then came the surprise. I quizzed the willing members (my kind son, who is beauty, was not wanting to participate, but still saw I was expressing his goodness) to see how many definitions of the word beauty they could remember. This was fun, and as a result of paying more attention to the word, it became more intense. Imagine waking up in the morning reading "I am beauty," and "I am intensely pleasing," and repeating this a number of times during the day. This continued as I covered the tree with seven different meanings, including those found for beauty. Then I extended my knowledge to include the definitions of some of the words found to define beauty or beautiful. For example, I extended my definitions to include the investigation of the words "remarkable," "superior," "aesthetic," "deep," and "excellent." At the end of the week, my family, who is, not expected to be, beauty, is also, as cited in *Webster's College Dictionary*, deep, not superficial; of outstanding quality; remarkably excellent; of superior merit; notably and unusually kind; thinking, feeling and perceiving. These are intensified as they are affirmed through the "I Am" approach, therefore suggesting they are within the spirit now and do not need to be taught or expected. What a beautiful sense of calm that has brought us so much happiness.

What followed each new word was the placement of the previous week's word meanings in a scrapbook called "Our Family's Life in Pieces." I did not want anyone to forget what made up our family tree, and creating a memory book provided the opportunity to look back and reflect on our life and family. This is only one activity of many reflecting the message of hope and love in "A Life in Pieces."

What an enlightening experience. Through the many constructed masterpieces built to understand, in great detail, words of excellence, I now realize that we would not have achieved peace using any therapy or process delving into our problems. We had to leave the problems completely out of our marriage, then calm our hearts and minds to re-engage and ignite our feelings for each other through words of virtue, which were ready to explode from within.

This truth, which transcends explanation as it penetrates through the very depths of one's soul, led me to the greatest irony of all: contrary to popular belief, I admit I am not one to infect the spirit of children with my behavior and expectations. If I could not work magic rearing an adult into a more caring and compassionate being, I could not succeed in doing so with a child. All I needed to know was that the soul and spirit of a child are like mine, no matter the difference in age. Thus the paradox, the contradiction, the ironic process that is creating outcomes for others and myself that are not expected—allow children to be who they are. In intensifying their excellence, it is they who will bring peace to this world. I am most ecstatic when I envision junior high and high school students engaging in their "Life in Pieces," exploring their individual hearts and minds to help them create a process of peace for their school, families and communities. I am curious and anxious to witness the process all these children (yes, even the ones who are "bad") will implement to help solidify peace for the world as they know it. I believe even young children are ready and waiting to make this world a peaceful place for all. I am waiting for all children, any age, to guide me; for they know the way. To them, and also to me, it is so simple. Yet, everything is so complicated in the world, with continuous research into the reasons for existing pain, confusion, depression, abuse, war, et cetera. We keep searching for answers to solidify peace, yet ironically, we have known the answers for a long time, we just choose to ignore them. We, as a world, do not take the time to think about what has been discovered about the spirit of man, therefore we act with limited intellectual engagement and blame most of the problems in our life on humans who are not allowed to fight back: the children.

The answer is to take care of children, for it is they who will lead us to peace.

CHAPTER SIX

ADULTS: THE NON-THINKERS

Take care of children and they will lead us to peace. This is my beautiful truth. The world claims a desire to care for the children and provide them with a life of calm and safety. It sounds so simple. There should be nothing more important, as children will tell us as well. Yet, we continue to fail at this critical task. I believe it is this inability of the grown-ups in the world to offer a safe haven for our offspring that interferes most in the process to peace in any relationship. One barrier that interferes with solidifying peace in homes, schools, communities and societies is the fact that society labels children as problem-makers, therefore concentrating most of the effort towards improving humanity on improving, or breaking and changing children, not grown-ups. This is a non-thinking solution to peace, since adults make up most of the world's population; they must obviously be responsible for much of the world's problems. Another non-thinking issue is the fact that society places the responsibility of ridding the world of the problems they think children create on adults, who are themselves very ineffective as builders of peace and respect. They lack the very skills they attempt to teach children: kindness; equality, compassion, and so on. Success cannot abound when these important truths are ignored. Peaceful solutions to any relationship are unlikely.

This chapter, and the next, were the most difficult to investigate and write because I concentrated on the failures of the adult population that contribute to the abuse and bullying of our vulnerable young. I am saddened, confused and repulsed by the enormity of these failures. For example, it is a fact that more children are born addicted to drugs and affected by alcohol than ever before. This caus-es unwanted physiological, physical and psychological disabilities that can last a lifetime and negatively affect how others feel towards this child victim. This is the fault of the mother, not the child. Child porn is a growing business, now recruiting newborns into its seedy and dis-gusting underworld of internet porn. This has been created by adults, not children, who have a demand and a need for sex with children. It is also created by adult greed, where the level of advertising any suc-cessful product or service, like sex, increases when there is an increase in profits. It does not matter that compassion and any sense of humane treatment is eliminated. It is also a fact that children living in meth homes are on the rise due to the addiction of adults, not chil-dren. In these homes, children are often raised in environments like garbage dumps, by adults who have lost all morals and judgment, openly abusing their children physically, emotionally, and/or sexual-ly. Further more, it is known that corporal punishment of children who do not follow rules is still present in many schools and homes. In these environments, the adults believe this aversive punishment is justified and completely necessary in order to make a child well-behaved, and better able to follow every command of the adult, no matter how impossible it is to do so.

These failures are just a few of many that infect the lives of chil-dren with such repercussions as brain damage, emotional damage and/or moral death. This affects the child's ability to function appro-priately. Inappropriate behaviors, like impulsiveness, inattention, and aggression, to name only a few, are displayed by children born addict-ed, abused, living in meth homes, et cetera. These behaviors, created by the conditions of the environments that house the children, make relationships with adults difficult, and patience can easily run thin to a point where it is deemed necessary to label some children for mis-behaving, medicate them, and obsess over teaching them to behave appropriately. These are not examples of adults acting to better the child or mankind. These are examples of adults who are not thinking, thus causing the very problems the world so wants to eliminate.

No matter the condition of the home, school, or daycare that children are housed in, many grown-ups obsessively engage in mod-ern-day child-rearing practices (social skills training) to make children into the decent adults they think they should be. I am shocked that abused children, who live in environments where they are sworn at, hit, perhaps even hated, get timed-out for such things as assuming to not follow the rules (to be kind), not thinking before acting out (do not use bad language), and not behaving properly (must not hit). This causes endless despair and confusion in children, as they are expected to understand and follow through with commands that adults in their life do not follow. It all adds up to an excessive amount of moral teaching from non-thinking grown-ups who have not yet themselves achieved success in these areas.

I give credit to those adults who understand and worry about the chaos and confusion in the world and conclude that change is necessary and must happen now. Unfortunately, the credit stops there. Those very adults may not think it is they who must change or become humbled: a non-thinking conclusion. Adult "social skills" do not exist. These are meant only for children and adults believe it is children who will some time in some generation solve all the world problems, when they become adults themselves. Modern day child-rearing practices are implemented to satisfy the assumption that they help children learn how to bring peace to the world and, ironically, the children are assumed to be taught humility and equality by the very adults who have caused the world's chaos. The following is how I imagine the adult brain is thinking (or not thinking):

1. There are wars in the world. These must stop, so we have to teach children to be kind to one another.
2. There is sexual, physical and moral abuse in abundance in the world. This must stop, so we have to teach children to be empathetic and not get angry. At the very least, we adults must train them to manage their anger.
3. There is stealing and violence in the world. This must stop, so we have to teach children to think before they act and think about the consequences of their actions.
4. There is bias and racism in the world. This must stop, so we have to teach children to be accepting of differences and become aware of individuality.

When I started to reason and attempt to make more rational decisions, such as eliminating ignorance and assumption and dissecting obvious ironies, I gained insight into the world's "Life in Pieces." I came to intellectualize the fact that we, as grown-ups, tend not to think before we act. It is necessary to stop abuse of any kind in the world, but there can be no elimination of injustice if adults do not look to question change themselves. Adults create wars because of adults' selfishness, self-righteousness, control and/or revenge. These are only a few of the many reasons used to justify war. Adults destroy the innocence of children because they engage unwilling children in despicable activities. And yet it is the children who are consumed by the adult obsession to train them into the adults that they are not. Thus the irony: we must stop the impossible task of teaching social skills to children in order to eliminate problems adults have created and continue to engage in. Think about this: children, especially the very young, have nothing to do with the horrors and injustices that are happening in the world or in relationships. We do not need to blame children for any violence; adults fulfill this role very well. There is a pandemic of disrespect and apathy everywhere, happening in the absence of children. It is not children who are void of excellence, nor is it children who are causing the world's problems.

As I gained feeling and insight into this truth, I came to understand that children also feel this reality and sense its ludicrousness. Children are peaceful beings. A child is ready to live with already existing virtues. They are then confused by the obsessive instruction on how to behave and interact with others. Imagine a lesson on kindness when you already are kind. It is confusing to know what is being expected of oneself when you are already in possession of necessary and appropriate behaviors. It is therefore best to leave children alone, not insulted nor humiliated in spirit. Think for a moment. We, the grown-ups, do not like to be told we lack the morals necessary to be productive human beings. If we are so accused, we feel insulted and become defensive. Adults are offended by any assumption that they are not interacting or behaving properly in their families or workplaces. It is appropriate then to place your heart in the feelings and emotions you remember from your childhood, then follow with clear thinking about what we, as grown-ups, put our children through. Think clearly about your, and also their, ability to detect hypocrisy. Think clearly about natural reactions to insult. Now place yourself in the heart of the following truths that created "A Life in Pieces."

Please give this some thought because it will change your life.

1. Morals, virtues, and values are so critical in the quest for equality and peace, and so personal to each individual, that no man or woman on earth can possibly teach them. They already exist within.
2. Morals, virtues, and values are divinely given, a blessing for humans to enjoy.
3. Morals, virtues, and values are to be received gladly and openly (not ignored), free of charge or commitment, by those who are in your life.
4. Morals, virtues and values are to be intensified and guided (not taught) upon conception; the spirit becomes exalted.
5. Life begins in uteri with "I am all I need to be."

A lot of thinking went into my program at the time these truths were recorded on paper and presented orally. I now want to engage you in an activity of deep thinking, beginning by encouraging you to question if it is worth believing that children of the world are immoral, unproductive, selfish, and unreasonable—to name only a few of the labels used by grown-ups to describe children. Engage your brain and question the consequences of ignoring the great virtues instilled within our spirit at the time of conception, then contemplate if it is worth ignoring the excellence given to the human race by a much grander being, one that many call God. Think please....

A message from somewhere above, from a creator far greater than any human.

Is It Worth It?

...if you, my grown-up child, do not see the radiance, brilliance, kindness and warmth I have given freely to you in heart and mind.

...if you feel it is your right to judge, from poor to excellent, what I have made in human body and spirit, thus creating the future by your goals, not the goals of the divine.

...if you engage in ignorance, and ignore all that I produce in excellence that allows you to bond easily with all the world's children.

Because if you do ....

You will have a world built by man, with labels that are assuming and actions that are misinterpreted, due to a lack of knowledge concerning the pieces of our souls.

You will be surprised at the rebellious nature of children who feel they can no longer live up to your expectations, as they realize what I have created in them is never good enough for your perfection.

You will continue to believe that a child has no skills in which to live gracefully, and you will see that the future cannot cope.

This world will not find the peace that is at its fingertips.

Stop! Listen! Think, before it is too late!

Fold up the social skills and your interpretation of moral productivity, for rectitude exists within us all. You do not have to teach the essentials of life for this is too difficult, even impossible.

Children engrossed in beauty sit before you, ready to live. All my children, with their own unique souls, are kind and fair; bright and pleasing; wanting and innocent.

They are your treasure and your future.

So, I need to know one thing. Understanding the aftermath of ignorance, and the need to control....

Is It Worth It?

CHAPTER SEVEN

IS IT WORTH IT?

No benefits derive from ignoring innate goodness, nor from engaging in either ignorance or control. These are two negative traits displayed by adults when life is devoid of the conscious exploration of God's free virtues. Because it is not worth it to live a life void of exemplifying goodness (especially that of a child), I have distanced myself from personal or professional conversations about children described as irritating, manipulative, oppositional, super-brat, et cetera. I have thankfully developed a program that ensures that the implementation of more positive, truthful descriptions of children/students, like eagerness, excitement, happiness, sadness, and fear, are contemplated first before the label Attention Deficit Disorder (ADD) and/or Attention Deficit Hyperactivity Disorder (ADHD) is attached to any child. I have thankfully developed an assessment process that steers away from worthless and tragic labels like Conduct Disorder (CD) and Oppositional Defiance Disorder (ODD). These labels are ignorant and non-thinking, and they can be devastating. It has been proven that children labeled as CD or ODD because, for example they do not follow the rules, are disengaged, do not listen and/or do not share, are more likely as they get older to become delinquent, addicted, violent, depressed and even suicidal. It is impossible for me to consider such a life for any child. Many experts are concerned about such consequences for children labeled as CD and ODD, and have concluded that by catching bad behaviors characterized in these children, we, the perfect adults, can make the inappropriate behaviors go away. The truth is, I believe this will not, and does not, work. Knowing this is worth it.

I discovered the reverse to be true as I analyzed what I determine to be the over-used practice of labeling children at any age. My results revealed that many, if not most, children are not CD or ODD, thus causing them to exhibit bad and inappropriate behaviors. Many situations in a child's life can cause them to exhibit behaviors that seem inappropriate to an adult, especially one living a narrow existence with children that equates the quiet child as being the good child, and the loud, hyper child, as the bad. A child who exhibits behaviors that make an adult's life uneasy and stressful, is seen as unfit as he/she display behaviors that indicate he/she is incapable of handling a current situation, like school or daycare. This is most likely the stage before an assessment process begins. The child is incapable of functioning "appropriately," to adult standards, in a given situation, therefore there must be something wrong with the child. Tragically, such things as the grown-up's attitude toward the child, the (mis)interpretation of the child's actions, or the impossible expectations placed on the child are never considered nor assessed, yet each are very probable contributors to the child's inappropriate actions, if in fact they are inappropriate at all. A label will most likely be attached to the child after the assessment process is done, as the adult would say, to help change the child for their own good. For example, if the CD and/or ODD misbehaviors exhibited by a three-year-old are not changed (in the child or by the child), then that child may end up being a statistic of his diagnoses. Therefore, to help change the child, lessons come out stating all the rules the child must follow. There can be up to fifty or more social skills, rules and procedures for children to learn before the age of six; I know this because I have seen such programs. Along with these pages and pages of skills (that I repeat, very few, if any, adults can follow or have mastered), are consequences noted to ensure these children know what will happen to them if they disobey any rule. For many children/students, this sequence of events leads to a diagnosis. CD and ODD does not come first; individual adult interpretation and judgment from parents, foster parents, daycare staff and/or teachers do. This interpretation, describing innocent childhood behavior as bad, disordered, oppositional and/or defiant, changes the behavior towards, and feelings of, the adult to the child. As time goes on, other children may notice a negative relationship brewing, and may also begin to treat the child in a negative way. I have witnessed this on too many occasions. For example, I have been in the presence of parents and teachers who openly express their dislike towards rambunctious young boys who are hyper in class and more aggressive at recess. The boys find it difficult to: sit still (rule #1-sit still); pay attention and not interrupt (rule #2-look at the teacher as he/she is speaking and do not speak unless asked to); and not play-wrestle or engage in fight games, like the ones played by many boys for centuries and now seen in videos, movies or even cartoons (rule #3-do not touch another child; no tolerance for "aggression"). When asked to stop and behave, it is difficult for little boys because they are wired, at birth, with more energy than some of them can handle. This fact makes it difficult to comply with the first request to stop, as well as the second one, and perhaps numerous requests, thus creating frustration because of their "refusal" to listen to, respect, or co-operate with the adult. Tension between adult and child grows, causing more anxiety and hyperactivity in the child than existed before. Soon, a little boy will be seen as oppositional and defiant, creating a relationship of animosity between the child and the adult. Due to this animosity and the negative feelings that continue to grow, this child may never improve, and the adult jumps at the chance to assess and label the child to make him/her behave differently. To the child, this can, and likely will, be life-changing.

It is impossible to understand how a curious and rambunctious child can become, through adult interpretation, an oppositional and defiant child. Many label (or do not label) children because of their feelings and attitudes towards them. Too often children are labeled because of their inability to meet individual and personal expectations set by controlling adults, who themselves may have impossible expectations set by an education system, workloads, parenting, et cetera. Children are often not labeled because of a predisposition to bad behavior. Therefore, the tragic reality is that adults can be the cause of many children becoming delinquent, violent, addicted, depressed, and suicidal. Tragically, I fear this may be the path my little student, who was expelled from first grade, is headed. Kindness, calm, patience and caring for this child in kindergarten gave her so much peace and safety, and she was able to be herself. But obvious dislike, impatience and labeling by her first grade teacher caused the expulsion of this child. This is not a child with CD or ODD. This is a child held in contempt by one or more adults. This is a tiny, young, innocent girl opposing the unfair and unjust treatment towards her. I hope she remembers the beauty within her soul. I pray she recalls her excellent spirit, remembering her life puzzle filled with her virtuous qualities. Thankfully, there is an easy answer to a fulfilling, tranquil life for her, other children, and adults: as adults adopt a different approach, children will not be oppositional. If children are not interpreted as being oppositional, there will be no need to label them ODD or CD. Without labels, the negative, tragic consequences will be eliminated. Therefore, delinquency, bullying and violence, childhood addictions, depression, and suicide will be less of a worry because children will be happier living in environments where fairness, compassion, and safety explode.

There are many benefits to exploring and intensifying already existing virtues, just as there are many benefits implementing the process used in "A Life in Pieces." One of the most important is that it may save more than one child from living a tragic life or taking his/her own life. When it comes to defining character, it engages everyone who uses it 100 percent of the time. This fact is one of the most important recommendations of the United Nations Secretary General's report on the global violence against children ("The United Nations Secretary General's Study on Violence Against Children." Geneva. http://www.violencestudy.org. 20 November 2006). This report involves numerous agencies and persons, including a number of children themselves, who implore the involvement of children in everything that affects their lives. It can become a daily ritual to examine words of excellence with all children, no matter the age, leading to the approval (or disapproval) of the children when asked: "Are you kind?", "Are you fair?", and "Can you listen?" I do not contemplate the decision to involve children in this processes of peace, when screams of affirmation come back, saying, "I am kind, fair and I can listen!" This is so reaffirming to any child, especially to one who is mistreated by an adult. This can be the difference between a life of trauma and tragedy, and one of fulfillment and hope. Also, in accordance with the UN recommendations, if it is thought that any child is bad, irritating, or deviant, it is the obligation of the adult to inquire about the child's thoughts and opinions when using such words to describe him/her, engaging in questions such as, "Are you irritating?" or "Are you deviant?" What a relief to children to be given the opportunity to rebuke such accusations as "You are bad."

I have come to feel anguish when using words of discontent. I have thankfully come to offset such anguish by concentrating on words of beauty, words that become a daily ritual not only for children, but for spouses who proclaim their virtues of love, empathy and compassion. Sharing the exaltation of the spirit in both individuals can help to ensue a life of togetherness and prevent any dismembering or death of the family. It can become a daily ritual for the boss of a company to exclaim that the staff is productive because of their obvious respect toward each other and for the company. This can steer employees away from anger and depression because there will be a sense of pride and equality amongst the staff.

Enlisting the opinions of family members, students, staff, et cetera, is the best way to assure equality, respect and calm. With "A Life in Pieces," it is assured that all participants understand what character definition they are agreeing to because the definitions of each word have been explored together and can be inscribed on their life puzzle. In the case of children and labeling, this is the complete opposite to other processes where children have no idea they are being watched and assessed. In those cases, they have no say in how they are labeled, what they are labeled as, and why they are labeled. Think for a moment. Imagine that you are at work and your boss is secretly recording his/her personal opinion of who you are, how you act, and how you work. Imagine that what is being recorded on paper could change your life. Fellow employees may come to dislike you, your job responsibilities may change, and you may even get fired (expelled). At work one day—not aware this is going on—you are happy, eager, and energetic. The next day you go into the boss's office and you are given a label that is shocking and, you believe, not suited to the quality of character you possess, but there is nothing you can do to change it. The boss has been assessing your assumed inappropriate work ethics for awhile, and during this time he/she has been yelling reprimands and demands in front of other co-workers. There is a feeling of helplessness because you were not informed that you were being assessed, therefore you could not form an opinion about, nor argue against, any one of the character descriptions being used. In order to keep your employment, you have no choice but to comply to all your boss's expectations, even if they are inappropriate and/or impossible. You have no control over your life at work and this will have negative consequences at home. This is heartbreaking and unfair. This is not worth it.

It is worth displaying pieces of your life puzzle with character descriptions honoring benevolence. This changes the entire atmosphere of the classroom, the home, the workplace, and any other place, because the brain cannot concentrate on and intensify two opposite thoughts. There must be a choice between concentrating on opposition and all that equates to this word, or concentrating on all that is kind and cooperative. Telling another person, or even yourself, that "You are (I am) kind," pleases the brain, intensifies excellence, and breeds an atmosphere conducive to the true state of happiness. There are no negative feelings associated with words of excellence. It is that simple. This should be a daily ritual.

It took me many years to discover that daily displays of words intensifying goodness were worth it; that living superficially and uninformed was not. Prior to my awakening, I did not contemplate the consequences if beauty within was ignored. With regards to children, this allowed me to think that they were too young, and therefore incapable, of understanding peace; they were not all they needed to be. I concluded that my brilliant intervention would help them learn to be non-abusive, unbiased, et cetera. I implemented many programs to build understanding of moral values in my students and in my own children. There are multiple programs available to the public that instruct adults how to teach children of all ages to be acceptable human beings, so there was no problem finding a guide to assist with social skill building. I implemented more than one program, without thinking or researching them, and proceeded to teach and expect "proper" actions associated with each skill from all the students, whether the student was "normal," curious, rambunctious, or suffering from such disorders as FASD, Post-traumatic Stress Disorder (PTSD), ADD and/or ADHD. For many reasons this was, and obviously still is, inappropriate and not worth it. For example, one should never generalize expectations of children into one skill (rule) like: "You will sit, hands in lap, mouths quiet and feet under the desk." This is an impossible expectation that will create problems for many children as they attempt to succeed with the goal. It is a fact that children with FASD, ADHD, and children living in abuse, have a very difficult time sitting calmly and patiently, so it has been found that diversifying the rules and relaxing impossible expectations make it more compatible for these children to listen and learn. When they listen and learn because they are happy, there is no need or want to be assessing bad behaviors. Therefore, no unnecessary physiological and emotional harm will invade the life of the child or adult.

Many similar truths surfaced once I began to feel the injustice of my actions towards children. There was a need for a paradigm shift. There was a demand for an immediate awakening of my thought process, commanding me to research each skill from a number of social building programs more deeply. I came to realize that I was completely blind to the expectations outlined in each skill, and I began to read and pay conscious attention to each word used. I discovered that children who succeed in accomplishing these skills, such as treating others the way they want to be treated, remembering the rules and the consequences of their actions, avoiding uncontrollable negative behavior, and having empathy for others, should run our countries, be our bosses and our parents. Imagine every Prime Minister/President treating the population the way they want to be treated. What a sense of equality and importance, leading to greater emotional and economic production for, and from, the population. Imagine these country leaders remembering the consequences of inequality, for instance, as they allow the gap between rich and poor to grow in size. Nothing is gained providing guiltless opportunities for the discrimination of wealth amongst the population of any country and yet there is a greater divide today. More equality, in regards to wealth, decreases the divide amongst people, creating a more productive, peaceful existence. Imagine parents avoiding uncontrollable negative behaviors and the calm that would bring their children. The reality is that this is just imagining. Imagine teachers and daycare workers showing empathy for the feelings of all others. Seeing hurt in a child's eyes and understanding they, the adult, may be a part of the problem, would change a classroom. More equality in regards to the treatment of children leads to a sense of peace and improved social interactions, therefore a decrease in or even elimination of bullying and violence. This is the truth.

Chapter Eight

The Truth

If it were possible to teach life skills for all of mankind to master, our world would be more compassionate, empathetic and compatible. I believe it is not, in part, because adults disassociate themselves from not only the moral expectations, but also responsibility in most of the world's chaos. They engage in ignorance and allow a tormenting existence for many children as they:

1) ...expect too much from children, obsessing over procedures and rules that are impossible to follow. These rules are made and interpreted by individual adults who think differently from one another. They may be made by pedants who make inappropriate or excessive expectations, paying no attention to the important fact that children must be seen as individuals who are different in every aspect from adults. It is impossible to expect children to think and behave as adults do, especially when it is rare to find an adult who follows every skill expected of children. For example, with regards to children accepting (with calm and a smile on their face), the consequences of their bad behaviors that are defined by the interpretation of the child's action by the adult, imagine an adult having to accept that their actions are bad, even abusive towards children, and it is the child who gives the consequences for such behavior. I do not wonder if the grown-up would accept what they would call unnecessary discipline, and take the consequences calmly with a smile. It is my experience that nothing progressive or successful can come by promoting the training of social skills. They are unfair, unjust, and tormenting.

2) ...make problems where they need not exist. For example, unnecessarily assuming a child is insulted and hurt, thus needing

remorse and explanation from a fellow classmate who does not share or want to play. This builds unnecessary anxiety in a child's brain not yet ready to "read" hurt feelings and insults into their emotional vocabulary. Feelings like hurt and insult connect to the brain in a way that produces the flow of adrenaline, something the body can get addicted to if ignited too often. It is the excessive amount of adrenaline that causes non-thinking behaviors and impulsiveness, with the possibility of reaching a state of unrest even when surrounded by calm. Upon my discovery that the over-engagement of adrenaline causes much harm, I have learned to leave hypotheticals causing emotional uprisings out of any teaching. Unfortunately, many adults do not realize these negative consequences. At home, daycare, and/or school, parents and teachers use hypothetical scenarios often to explain things like unfair treatment and hurting each others' feelings. Children have lessons that describe in detail, the "mad" look, the "bad" actions, the "sad" feelings, et cetera. These hypotheticals make the brain aware of emotions and feelings that lead to insult, anger, sadness, and so on, thus creating a different dimension to a child's existence. It is no longer about "just being" in a calm and stressless environment with partners who are kind, heartful, and can be trusted not to intentionally hurt. It is a situation where thoughts of what others are not doing properly, or doing "meanly," are at the forefront of each day. This thinking about what can go wrong causes a constant flow of anxiety in both adult and child. It is by eliminating the need to teach problem situations before they exist, along with intensifying the reason why problems will not happen ("Recess will be great because everyone in the class is fair and kind"), that positive change will come to any relationship. Children are capable of working through emotions and relationships without much incidence. Grown-ups must allow this to happen without obsessive intervention.

3)...create the thought that one is never good enough. When emotions and behaviors, not feelings and intentions, are interpreted as problems, they are expressed through statements like:

> "That was not kind. That was not fair. What could you have done to make it better? How did it make your friend/partner feel? What do you need inside to be a better friend?"

In other words:

> "In my (mis)interpretation, you did something that
> you should not have. I now want you to spend time
> thinking about your actions that were bad (because
> why else would he/she be lectured), and then decide
> how to change yourself so you will not engage in this
> behavior again. When I am satisfied that you have
> made amends with your friend, I want you to accept
> your consequences (with a smile) and remember what
> we said so you do not repeat it."

The statements above are used to correct this behavior of a child
and they sadly create a sense of inadequacy in getting along with others and being a "good" person. Children perceive that they are inadequate, and they come to look for, and expect, training from an
adult—and even God—to achieve compassion and understanding.
For example, living with abuse in a home of alcoholism, drug addiction and domestic violence, and even at the time of homelessness, my
little student—who had by this time become a big part of our family—asked God to:

> "Make me a better person. Help me not to tattle-tale.
> Help me be a better friend. I do not want to be bad."

In truth, she does not need to engage in such thoughts because
she is the picture of beauty. "A Life in Pieces" took her away from
thinking she was inadequate, and together we created, and still create every time she spends the night, proud moments by sharing her
true character with God, expressing:

> "God, I am happy to tell you that I am kind and fair. I am
> sweet and agreeable, and I love to help others. I always
> want to make people happy. You can be very proud of me
> God, because I am good. I am all I need to be."

"I am all I need to be." Engaging in this positive program is
worth it. It allows the confident heart to guide intent and actions,

and eliminates most of what we would deem as problems. Growing in "A Life in Pieces" proves that most conflict that occurs, especially between children, is momentary, and the calm heart that now exists allows the natural tendency just to move on. It is not worth concentrating on the problem and encouraging the expression of emotions such as insult, anger and sadness, because this eventually leads to whining and problems that become, what adults would call, annoying and over-blown. All these cause frustration and anxiety that can grow into a feeling of being overwhelmed, for both the child and the adult. Neither the problem-maker, nor the accuser is safe from frustration when such emotions are present. Desperation eventually sets in, and what develops is a vicious cycle that leads to unnecessary trauma because it creates behaviors that grown-ups hate, such as opposition, impulsiveness and hyperactivity. In acts of desperation, violence can surface because the children, being in an extreme emotional state, lash out in frustration and can become "bullies." If persistent and obsessive moral training continues for desperate children, the situation will not change and will likely worsen for both adult and child. I no longer wonder why many children engage in gun violence, something that occurs in every country of the world and therefore must be looked at truthfully and realistically. It is critical to disengage from this cycle when children become desperate, before something tragic happens. It is time to look to the adult for a change in behavior, and time to tell the children that they are good enough. We must allow them to disconnect from torment, and express their natural feelings of discontent and opposition before it is too late. We need to understand the truth that in order to stop the increasing bullying and violence among our children, we the adults must first stop bullying and abusing them.

It is extremely senseless to ignore the consequences of adults' bullying behavior towards children. For example, grown-ups relentlessly follow some bad children to ensure that they will not engage in hurtful behaviors towards others. At a minimum, this habitual behavior may be non-consequential. Done in excess, it is bullying and tormenting because the child is constantly reprimanded and never feels good enough. I have witnessed such incidents on the school playground when one or more children are too often singled out in a short fifteen minute span. To decrease such bullying towards children, an adult just has to think of what it would be like to be followed excessively and nagged to ensure his/her unproductive, senseless interactions with children and/or adults is appropriate. This thinking could actually bring about a transformation in the adult community, if adults would find such an experiment worthy of participation. Unfortunately, it is often the practice of the adult population to ignore, no matter the consequences, the negative effects of its actions.

We cannot ignore the fact that discipline (bullying) by adults is regarded as acceptable and is often seen as necessary for the good of the child. As such, it is a remorseless act. We must pay attention to this hypocrisy, which is ignored, but very much alive. Adults permit themselves to judge children and other adults, disregarding and disrespecting those they deem unworthy of character, thus unworthy of companionship and friendship. They can label children and other adults as unkind, with no concern regarding these labels and no consequences or remorse for thinking such thoughts. Some adults will gladly estrange themselves from those they consider unkind. It is difficult for me to understand why children are not given the same opportunity to judge/examine another person's character and choose the relationship they will have with a particular grown-up or child. I was once told by a teacher and acquaintance: "There are teachers who will tell you children are not kind." This depressing statement was expressed with no sadness or contempt in his voice. I wonder how he would have reacted to a statement like: "There are students who will tell you that teachers are not kind."

"Children are not kind." How can anyone come to such a conclusion? I believe any adult who has this belief is unkind, non-thinking, and will likely have his/her feelings for an unkind child turn to contempt because one cannot be kind to, nor like, another they describe as unkind. In these situations, a child will not only have to repress any feelings of injustice that this attitude is causing, but will have little choice but to stay with this particular adult. When situations like these arise, many adults make these feelings known through seemingly guiltless, obvious displays of dislike toward some children.

This truth struck me hard at the funeral of the guardian (grandma) of an ex-pupil of mine who was nine years old at the time. As the two of us shared memories of Grandma, he cried as he said: "She worked hard to keep me safe." Safety in his tiny world, where he had been abused as a baby and placed into the guardianship of his grandmother, included her, his teachers (including myself), doctors, and psychiatrists. In truth, she had to keep him safe from some professionals who did not see into his spirit and labeled him as unkind, oppositional, and impossible to be around. This created interference with the mental and physical well-being of this child and his grandma, who were both unable to estrange themselves from these unjust behaviors, labeled by individuals who never saw this little boy possessing any goodness at all. In my kindergarten class he flourished, even after being taken off medication, to become a bright and caring boy. Immediately upon entering first grade he was diagnosed as a "problem child," spent half his time in the office for punishment, and was again put on medication. This was done with the permission of the guardian, upon the suggestion by his teacher who claimed that she was having trouble with him complying to the rules of first grade. I find it impossible to comprehend because he was compliant, socially acceptable, and gracious to me just a few months previous to this life-changing diagnosis. I conclude it was not the rules of first grade, but the rules and expectations of the teacher, who herself made it difficult for him to learn, or comply, because he was always anxious in her presence. It is a fact that children do not learn from those who dislike them. This boy was labeled as unkind by an unkind adult, and the child paid a hefty price. Eventually he was moved to another school that imposed the same impossible conditions. He was placed in three different schools his first-grade year, all with the same results. He was never allowed to find calm between schools, a very sad, but common occurrence for "problem" children. Many have become statistics in a system that labels a child not once, but numerous times in an attempt to cure behavior problems. This little student was placed on numerous medications in the attempt to "birth" him into the type of person the adult wanted him to be. This led him into a detox program at the age of eight.

Can you imagine this? How could this happen to a student of mine who I knew as an abused child? He was kind, giving, and bright, just wanting to be loved and happy. Echoing his spirit throughout the classroom in kindergarten provided calm and tranquility for Grandma and himself, a fact repeated often to me. Being attentive to my actions toward him, in order to avoid a sense of fear and anxiety, allowed him to be truly happy, and consequently built more love between he and his grandma. She never had to worry about him in my class. She never received phone calls detailing bad behaviors. He was never suspended, nor sent home early. This all happened the following year and this torment continued. Labeling him as an unkind child and obsessively nagging him and Grandma about his inappropriate behaviors changed everything for this small family. Pain and despair were constant. Trust in our system of professionals was gone. Sadly, at the time of his grandma's funeral, not one teacher or professional that this boy's new guardian was aware of shared any remorse for their negative and thoughtless actions and behaviors toward this young child. It is such a sad reality when unkind adults rule. Thankfully, he is living with a loving new family. What a relief.

Moments of relief come to remind me of the obvious beauty exemplifying many adults that I have met, or read about in my journey to a better life. Many want equality for children, and understand that it is children who can change this world. If they knew of a better way, I believe many adults would change. I believe that many, if not most adults want to see new attitudes toward all children, no matter what age. What instills this belief is:

1) The repeated fact that none of my workshop participants has been insulted or become offended by my program. They have shared thoughts and have used these to question themselves in regards to the way they teach and/or parent, and how they can feel differently in their relationships. Speaking confidently through the words of "A Life in Pieces" is calming to the mind, allowing for an examination of life to occur in a non-threatening manner. No one feels intimidated by any suggestion that they change their approach with children. The members of "A Life in Pieces" want to feel different; they do not have to. Upon completion of this peaceful seminar, the participants are genuinely satisfied, knowing they have been instructed in a concrete solution to deal with much of the frustration in the classroom and in their homes. There is no sense of disillusionment or confusion, feelings many, including myself, have at the completion of some of the "make the child better" workshops. "A Life in Pieces" is the end of my search. I no longer have to keep looking for answers to make children/students better; they are all they need to be. I want to thank

these participants for inspiring me with their obvious excitement in regards to contrary opinion and truths. They have proven to me that there are adults who want a different way to live in all their relationships, personal and professional. This is empowering.

2) There are many in this world who work day and night to protect children and their rights. I believe these adults, whose obsessive love for children is evident in everything they do, thrive on the realization of the "I am…" approach and the knowledge that children are simple, humble, unbiased, and non-violent. It is a blessing to see each new birth as a soul ready to bring peace to the world. These incredible grown-ups express their understanding of children through films, documentaries, movies, books, lectures, and more. They attempt, through the implementation of very vivid, fearless approaches, to cause a paradigm shift in a world with a large populace that remain uninterested. Some fight the courts and politicians in an attempt to make laws that disallow adults to man-handle and torture children. These incredible adults live daily with unfathomable facts like deaths, caused by adult staff members, of children who are housed in institutions like boot camps. They work tirelessly for this to never happen again; a hope that some feel at this time is not possible. Some adults risk their lives in an attempt to achieve equal rights, something the UN Declaration of Rights for Children wants to achieve, but obviously cannot ensure. This world is blessed with many parents and teachers who constantly intensify the excellence of children and attempt to overpower the contempt of many adults toward them. I am proud to have presented "A Life in Pieces" to caring individuals such as these, as it is a peaceful addition to their daily fight for justice and equality for all children.

Unfortunately, in our world we allow adults without a clean slate the right to develop rules and use labels that cause increasing frustration and anxiety. Many children who have been, and still are, emotionally, physically, and sexually abused, even brutalized by adults are often labeled as oppositional and defiant by their abuser, and others, for breaking rules, or in my words, opposing the abuse and fighting back. Opposition and defiance are traits hated by adults, and consequently affect the manner in which the child is treated. It is often the reason for increased frequency and severity of the abuse. What is ignored is the likely truth that in both peaceful and tormenting environments, children try to the best of their ability to comply with all rules, especially children living in abusive situations because of their sensitivity to yelling, nagging, desperation, and fear, all of which they want to eliminate from their life. Imagine the pain and confusion. Abuse is impulsive, uncontrolled, and confusing, so a child never really knows what to do to stop "it" from happening, because "it" is never the same, so "it" can never be clearly defined. What intensifies the pain and confusion is the fact that existing rules are not constant and, making it even worse, these rules are set to adult standards by adults using their grown-up brains. This is an impossible truth for children, especially those whom are punished severely for disobeying commands. It is a fact that the brain of an adult is different from that of a child, especially one tormented by abuse. For example, children's memory capacity is shorter and their brain is not capable of organizing information in the same manner in which an adults can. This fact worsens for children exposed to abuse. Because these are unknown and/or ignored facts, we allow ourselves, as grown-ups, to expect too much of the young. We make them remember numerous individual, personal rules and regulations along with reading, writing and arithmetic.

My wish is for adults to expect too much of themselves. Is it too much to ask adults to hear alarms go off signifying the need for change? We need a change in our interpretation of opposition, anger and deviance because words like these cause much of a child's frustrations and anxieties, which can lead to feelings of torment and trauma. Please hear me again as I stress that research shows the brain of a child is affected, and even altered, by trauma-causing events and environments, such as living in homes of alcoholic and abusive parents, or being around individuals who over-obsess about impossible rules for children to achieve. For example, children are not meant to possess an adult's interpretation of the principles of altruism because they do not have the pre-requisites nor the understanding to accomplish what we believe is suitable to such expectations. If they do not share, or want to play with another child, this is not a devastating sign that the child will turn out to be disrespectful, belligerent, or even violent. Children are kind and they do love, but by their own standards that they are physiologically able to succeed with. Expectations that are impossible and inappropriate increase non-compliant and oppositional behavior, increasing what the adult would see as the need for moral training for the child. This means more rules, causing more anxiety and more failure. In all the pain and confusion a child is experiencing, opposition and defiance are relevant, but not allowed. This is a fact that disturbs and confuses me because adult victims of abuse and trauma are encouraged to oppose any mistreatment and seek shelter away from pain. It is critical that children be allowed to scream out their indignation and injustice caused by inappropriate rules and labels without being called bad. It is important to pay attention. A child should feel safe to tell you, the adult, what to do to make any situation better.

Acknowledging and paying close attention to facts that can decrease trauma and stress is positive in any situation. In doing so, the environment is conducive to better learning because the child can listen more attentively when feeling calmer inside and the brain is physiologically better equipped to recall what it has been told. These are two points that make both the teacher/parent, and student/child happy. An increase in positive social interactions and relationships is more likely to occur when environments are altered to work with the capabilities of children and their hearts and minds. When adults delve into the hearts and minds of children, they are reigniting the feelings and emotions they experienced as young newcomers to the world. In essence, working with a child's spirit is understanding one's own; one reaches a sense of clarity.

CHAPTER NINE

LIVING WITH ALL MY SENSES

I wish for everyone to experience the translucence I have found in my awakening. I now integrate all my senses into every part of each day as I immerse myself in "A Life in Pieces." My eyes have been opened to very important facts about life, facts that have changed me and brought me peace. One example of change comes from the realization that it is impossible for me to know exactly what is happening in a child's life, or anyone else's outside my immediate relationships with family. Therefore it is impossible for me to judge the actions of almost everyone and interpret their intentions. This is because, more often than not, I do not know circumstances preceding an act, which makes it inappropriate for me to think I am right in my interpretation of a behavior. A simple example that awakened me to this truth is the sharing, or fighting over, of toys between children. Before I implemented "A Life in Pieces" into my everyday thinking and attitudes, I intervened when my students, or my own children, were involved in a tug-of-war over a favorite toy. I never once thought my judgment could be/was biased due to the fact I did not see what preceded the incident, therefore I never stopped to think that how my decision was made, as to who got the toy in the end, was unfair. I realize now that my decision was based largely on my belief that one of the children involved in the incident was more of a troublemaker in the class, or at home, therefore was the troublemaker in this instance. I recall, sadly, to have given the toy to the one who in my mind was good most of the time. This was, and is wrong. This was, and is frustrating and insulting to the child(ren). The phrases that redirected this inappropriate behavior of mine, like "You students are all fair, so I know you can share," made me realize that if I did not see what instigated an incident between two equally kind classmates (because they are), I could not possibly know who had the toy first, who took the toy from who, nor who had the toy the longest. I began to feel at peace when I acknowledged all children are capable of fairness, and, conversely, of childlike selfishness. More importantly, all children are capable of handling situations by themselves. What a moment of clarity. I was willingly absorbed into a brand new life, a brand new reality. I was never going to be the same.

What is reality? That preconception, often leading to misinterpretation, is a common practice among adults, and it seems unimportant to investigate or change it. Of course this is wrong. For instance, it may be thought that it is inconsequential to a young boy if a preconceived notion of him being wild and aggressive affects how a teacher will interpret his behavior and character. We, as adults, believe children are resilient to such practices, even if these notions and consequent attitudes toward a child lead to insult and humiliation. This thought of resilience is untrue for both children and adults. Everything is of consequence when preconceptions of character lead to misinterpretation of the intent of one's actions and words, because intentions come from the heart, and most times fair and happy outcomes are intended. I changed my interactions with children once I understood.

What is my passion for change? Living many years with others misinterpreting my intentions and behaviors (actions), thus leading to accusations that were unfounded and destructive, almost destroying our family unit. When love and fairness literally gush out of every pore of one's body to guide harmony in relationships, it is shocking when this beauty is misinterpreted for various reasons, or sometimes for no reason at all. Eventually, this shock turned to hopelessness and desperation within me as I realized that no matter how hard I attempted to show cooperation and compassion, all the while living in silence with injustice, there was no change. This felt like "hell." One of the greatest successes of "A Life in Pieces" is the fact that it got me out of this desperate place, ironically a place I am now thankful for because it changed my life. As a result, I am very aware of preconceived ideas and attitudes and how destructive they can be, and I do not wish them on anyone, especially children. I do not want anyone to feel the genuine hurt, insult, desperation, and justifiable anger this causes. Engaging in the unfair practice of preconception, that contributes to unjust attitudes and behaviors through the resulting misinterpretation of character, can destroy any child or adult. To any adult trapped under these circumstances, I want to tell you I understand and I feel your pain, and, at the same time, your strength to keep going. This book and my program have reached adults who have suffered injustice, and they have expressed their appreciation in its honesty. They have also been thankful to hear words shared by one who has suffered. They have said they themselves have found some peace because of it. I am now emotionally attached forever with those who suffer needlessly.

Thankfully, today my emotions never reach a level that is impossible to handle because I remember the intense beauty intensified in the heart of those now in my life. How relaxing. In this state of mind and body, I am not worried that anxiety and annoyance will surface, thus making it hard to bond with some children and adults. I do not use labels like "deviant," "oppositional" and "bad," therefore I eliminate the strong emotions that are attached to such devilish character. I do not lecture on the expectation of kindness, but instead I intensify this virtue, affirming each day, "I am kind" and "You are kind." I am happy, surrounded in warmth in my new reality.

I am joyous to have discovered that "A Life in Pieces" prevents unnecessary and unjust discipline, thus decreasing and even preventing destructive feelings in children. The following things are avoided: Firstly, feelings of anxiety. Children will no longer expect that discipline will rein down on them with no indication of when, or for what reason, because these fluctuate; secondly, the feeling of frustration, because play and/or work will rarely be interrupted with a command to change what a child is doing because of a misinterpretation that he/she has not followed the rules; and thirdly, the tormenting feeling of desperation, because there will no longer be the many wrongful accusations (the children know what happened) and unfair discipline, thus eliminating the feeling inside the child that he/she is disliked. I have been told stories of children being in the vicinity of a toy that falls off the shelf in a store and the immediate reaction of that child is to exclaim, "I did not do that," without even being accused. This defensive response is a reaction to the always present interpretation and wrongful accusation that the child has done something wrong. What a sad and unjust reality that is so easy to change. We must learn to interpret the actions of others only when the whole scenario is played out before us in plain view and there is no mistaking what has occurred.

I am thankful that my senses and intuition awakened me to the negative consequences of common discipline practices, thus engaging me in the exploration and discovery of a different approach to use when redirecting the behavior of children/students. To begin with, I do not use the word "discipline," as it has a negative connotation and suggests training a person to act in accordance to given rules. If there are behaviors to modify or eliminate, for example hitting other classmates, I use the word "awareness," not "discipline," as it is less controlling and stressful. This is such a successful step when redirecting negative behaviors that I had been asked by other teachers to engage in the process with their students, even if I was not the observer nor the accuser of inappropriate behavior. Follow me through this awareness from the classroom.

The process involved in "A Life in Pieces" starts with the retrieval of the words of virtue that have been investigated, intensified, then written on the classroom life tool: the puzzle. Remember, these words that the students can see and touch daily have come to characterize each one of them; they are proud to be labeled with words of excellence. Once the puzzle is in my arms and held for all to see, the students involved in an inappropriate display of behavior, and myself, repeat the words that have been written on the puzzle pieces, followed by questions like: "Are you kind?" and "Are you fair?" to which the children answer "yes," because these words are now known to exist within. I then proceed to ask the students involved if what they did was kind ("no") and fair ("no"). The character traits that were missing at the time of the incident are then removed from the conjoined pieces and the children see they are not together; there are pieces missing from their heart. The next step is to work towards rejoining the pieces by the end of the day, at which time the children are reminded that their excellent qualities will not allow a repeat of the behavior that occurred earlier on. What is the awareness achieved? The children are kind, fair, and helpful, therefore will hopefully not engage in hurtful behavior again. They redirect their thinking and actions because they are hurt inside when pieces of themselves are removed. What a success it is to witness children feeling sad and anxious when pieces of their heart and character are apart. This is true sympathy and empathy. I witnessed a group of children feel genuine remorse due to the fact that they did not like a piece of their heart missing; it was a depressing reality they wanted changed. The children did not change their behavior because they had to and/or because they may be punished, they changed because they wanted to. "A Life in Pieces" accomplishes that.

The students in my class glowed and rejoiced when the thirteen words describing themselves were cemented onto our classroom puzzle. Using positive affirmations to make children aware of redirecting behavior is very successful and long-lasting. One morning, I had a group of such students arriving to school on the bus. The driver had indicated to me that a group of eight children were unsafe, loud and saying mean words to each other. As soon as I entered the class, I sought out the eight students, picked up our life puzzle, and proceeded to discuss the issues that had occurred on the bus that morning. I asked the students what happened on the bus (since I was not there), and they admitted to all the behaviors the driver was concerned with. These included a problem with one boy who repeatedly took off his seatbelt, more than one child screaming, and one child using inappropriate language. After the students relived the morning events, I emphasized the puzzle pieces "kind," "fair," and "bright" and asked the students if their behavior reflected these virtues ("no"), then proceeded to remove them. Then I asked the students to listen as I sang a tune and implemented these missing words of excellence that they were so proud to possess.

> "You are kind and you know it so you say nice words.
> You are gentle and you know it so you touch nice.
> You are pleasing to be around and you want everyone
> to know this.
> You are bright and you know it, so you listen to the
> driver."

After I sang this tune, I asked the students to join me in singing because I wanted them to feel the message these words were giving. After the awareness lesson (the reminder that they are virtuous and this is why they do not behave in the manner in which they did), I remind-ed the group that we will try real hard to rejoin the pieces by the end of the day. I also mentioned that I would be having a meeting with the driver the next morning to ask how everyone behaved. The next morn-ing, I was greeted by a smiling driver who glowingly praised the stu-dents, calling them angels. In the class, the children were so happy to know they were pieced together. There were no incidences on the bus for these students, not only that morning, but for the rest of the morn-ings in the school year. There was success for more than one reason:

1) No stress was created, as the words spoken improved their inappropriate behavior by exclaiming they are all that is good. No words to the contrary were used.

2) I did not have to wonder, or worry about, what kind of morn-ing the students had prior to coming to school, thinking my disci-pline might torment them even more. If a child was scared, anxious or hyper-active because of being bullied at home, abused by a parent or sibling, sworn at because it was getting late, woken up by a parent hung-over from a binge the night before, or fearful that the police may come to break up a domestic incident, my approach to redirec-tion was not going to add to their trauma; in essence, it was going to de-stress the students. It was necessary for me to worry about my approach with the students that I taught because one or more of these scenarios was a reality. I engaged in an awareness approach that solidified that they are all that is good. If the students expected rep-rimand, they did not get it.

3) I asked the children for an explanation about the morning's events so I did not have to (mis)interpret what happened on the bus. Because of this approach, the students knew I was not "siding" with the driver.

4) This awareness (discipline) creates calm, allowing the brain to retain the information given, therefore ensuring long-term success. This awareness made the students so proud, and each day as they stepped off the bus they shared their pride, exclaiming: "Lana I kept my seatbelt on," "Lana I spoke nicely today," and "Lana I listened to the driver."

The students in my class were misty-eyed and upset if there was an issue that caused a piece(s) of their character puzzle to be removed. Because the process of awareness using "A Life in Pieces" creates real remorse, it ushers in a change in behavior that is long-lasting. Another morning on the bus a couple of students were bullying another child, calling him names and laughing at him. It was the driver who asked that I address these issues as they were not only unkind, they were also unsafe. So, that morning I asked the three boys to leave the classroom to talk to me. I had our classroom puzzle in my possession, and immediately asked the boys what occurred on the bus that morning. I then reacquainted (made aware) the boys with the investigated words discussed thus far. After I reminded the three boys that they are kind, they are warm, and they make me smile, I asked the bullied child to express the feelings that were the direct result of the actions of his classmates. After this was shared, I asked his two classmates if what they did was kind ("no"), fair"(no), or heartful ("no"). I also asked if they would like their mothers called to be told their boys had a cold heart. They said no, with a crushed look on their faces because they did not want their benevolent character torn apart. This was not because they were afraid of punishment, but because they wanted to be kind. The pieces with inscribed words of virtue were then removed with the understanding they could be replaced at the end of the day, depending on the boys' actions (I knew they would achieve this goal). When it was time to go home, pieces all intact, I reminded the boys to stay on the bus the next morning, as I would be there to meet with them and the driver to find out how the bus ride was. The next morning, I entered the bus and to my delight, I was told that the boys were great, making the bus ride to school pleasant and safe. I looked into beaming, proud eyes and I almost cried. I told them both that I knew they were kind and that their greatness was no surprise. I told them they had made me smile, as they were thinking of all their schoolmates on the bus that morning. As we were ready to go into school, one of the boys shared a beautiful truth that brought back all the reasons for the creation of "A Life in Pieces." He brought a book from home that morning to read to the classmate he bullied the day before. It was he who initiated this warmth, asking his classmate to sit by him so he could share the book.

It was becoming very clear that, due to the selfless pride felt when connected to character traits like pleasant, compassionate, and respectful, it broke the hearts of my students to see the pieces of their life puzzle removed. This intensified the chosen words one connects to in "A Life in Pieces." Then, concentrating on making this a daily ritual, children cemented in their hearts that they are all that is excellent. This feeling of awareness, respect, happiness, and so much more extended beyond the classroom. The families of the students were witnessing changes in their children at home. Mothers explained that their children were transformed, with aggression down and more compassion shown. I am elated because everyone is a winner using a program that expresses confidence in every child.

It is with great satisfaction and gladness to have realized that this positive atmosphere, created with "A Life in Pieces," can allow the mind and heart of any child to escape the effects of traumatizing emotions that develop because of tormenting and abusive situations. My heart is so calm at the end of the day when I realize children can go home knowing they are kind and warm, no matter what anyone tells them. What I give to them as I intensify their spirit will make a huge difference in their lives. Imagine if all teachers instilled this beauty in their students. Imagine if all parents instilled this beauty in their children. There would be a decrease in the most horrific consequences resulting from children being abused and bullied. These consequences are bullying by the child, violence by the child, depression in the child, childhood and juvenile delinquency, and suicide. Children will not partake in violence because desperation is not possible. Children know they are kind, and when kindness prevails, violence and bullying are non-existent. Children will not become depressed because they will not be desperate. It is that simple.

Readers, I believe you can now understand why it is so easy for me to eliminate negative words when relating to, and describing, children. I no longer see a child's anger and opposition as a problem of disregard toward the older generation, because interestingly, through the investigation of these words, I discovered that both actions can be justifiable. A child is justified in opposing behaviors that are mean and rules that are worthless. A child should oppose and be angry with inaccurate accusations; adults always feel the necessity to do so. Most importantly, everyone is justified when defending honest, harmless intentions. I fully understand that if I demand something that feels worthless in meaning, like intervening and interfering in play because I did not see sharing (in my view), a child will oppose it. It is now easy for me to let go of control and constantly challenge myself to understand life through words that define heart and soul. Since children are respectful and concerned, I look to myself to change when a child is upset. A child no longer needs to repress feelings when in my presence. There is a real sense of calm in all persons when opportunity presents itself to reveal our true feelings with no fear of reprisal. This is the path to peace and true happiness. In the process of attempting to intensify the goodness in children, I gained a new life. It is so simple.

Repeatedly throughout my message I have proclaimed my true happiness, clarity, and relief found through "A Life in Pieces." What a joy it is to experience a new life inspired by children. I pray I do them justice and I hope I make a difference.

I now invite every child and adult to feel and understand themselves through the thirteen first-class words of character and inner-beauty that are coming. I close my eyes for each word and envision answers as to why we are, or are not, certain definitions of virtue. For example, I see a child scream in delight that she is good. She knows this for so many reasons: one, being that she wants to make all people happy; two, she is always concerned with doing what is right; and three, she is concerned with the decencies of her behavior. She is not defiant, because her kindness disallows any defiant behavior.

Everyone will know when they live by the words of virtue and excellence because screams of divine affirmation will echo through homes, schools, neighborhoods and work places. Peace will greet you in the morning and lay you to sleep at night. Empathy and sympathy will be a part of daily rituals, allowing for sensitive and safe relationships. It is the emotional experience and feeling I received from each of these words that led me to the decision to find forgiveness in my soul for the pain I caused children before I found "A Life in Pieces." I want every child who has ever been in my care to understand they were not, and are not, bad.

Along with words of beauty, I have defined thirteen opposing "names" found in the black hole. I cry when I hear that these words are used to describe children. I cry because I once used some of these words when describing my students. I now exclaim that these word descriptions are not suitable for any child, nor many adults. You will know when you live in these words that are demeaning, insulting and despairing. Screams of rage, fits of anger, and tears of sadness will filter through homes, schools, neighborhoods, and workplaces. Desperation will prevail and stress leave will never become a term of the past. Be determined to eliminate these from your character descriptions. Read what is not, then throw these away.

Regarding the following words and definitions found in Chapter 11:

1) The definitions (from *Webster's College Dictionary*) changed my approach in regards to educating (guiding), and living, not only with children, but all others in my life. It all began with the written definitions of the words found in the dictionary, then went beyond the collection of letters into deep concentration to truly feel what they were trying to tell me. For example, good symbolizes moral virtuosity, two words I continued to explore, leading me to the words "kind" and "respect," which helped me discover "warm" and "cozy." Before long, good symbolized greatness and felt warm and cozy. Randomly, throughout each dialogue, I implemented words found from each definition. In this way I can build your trust that what is being communicated is not made up; it is not an imaginative dialogue. Some words used in the following chapter, such as "virtuosity," "disapproving," and "dispassionate," are uncommon for childhood dialogue and activities. I do not want you to be alarmed by my use of complex (adult) words because these are not meant to, but can be, used as an activity for the children/students. They are meant to give a clearer, more professional understanding of what is being felt when connecting a word to our souls. It is time that we genuinely say what we mean. Feel free to smile as I connect positive affirmations to understanding from within, and frown at the dislikable feeling created in the same way, while using negative affirmations. The following commentary is to help all readers understand how/why our hearts feel what others cannot see and the reasons why intentions behind reactions are genuine and important to listen to. This dialogue can be a private moment shared between you and me.

2) I speak the affirmations, both positive and negative, through the heart of all people, including infants, but I use words an adult can understand. Please hear children in these messages, for they are speaking to you with feelings that live within all of us from the time of birth. Please place yourself in the "I Am" affirmations, permitting happiness. Also place yourself in the "I Am Not" affirmations,

creating despair. Please imagine you are the children as you bring the child that is within you to life, helping you understand feelings and emotions that are sometimes hard to put into words, no matter one's age. For example, a kind child whose character is misinterpreted as being annoying and oppositional, may show helplessness through tears or may express anger while opposing wrongful convictions. In the same sense, a women who is abused, accused of the inability to parent, to care, perhaps to work, will also feel helpless and will likely shed many silent tears. Perhaps this could lead to outbursts which oppose the injustice. The words of acceptance and opposition both come from one's heart and the innate ability to feel.

3) I speak so much of children because it is easily forgotten that they are literally our future. We have created a world where our future generation is not used to, nor asked to, open up with genuine emotions and feelings. There is a tendency for adults to expect from children what they want to hear, not what the child needs to say. This causes a very unhappy existence. We, the grown-ups, must make our children happy. Use the following words, envisioning a child and yourself expressing words associated with moral excellence, and feel the warmth. This will help create a true sense of happiness within yourself and in your relationships, which then can change the future.

4) Repeat and intensity all the positive affirmations such as "I am helpful." These are not only the virtues of children, they are your virtues too! I include one or two examples to defend the given character descriptions, but there are many more. For instance, a child claiming to be eager and not disruptive or defiant as interpreted by an adult, can defend this truth because he/she knows the feeling inside of being earnest and joyful. This causes moments of irresistible impulsiveness that, to the child, is a display of happiness, not an act of deviance. Think of more examples of why you believe these words of excellence exist within our hearts and spirits. Begin these affirmations with "I Am..."

5) Be reluctant, and even refuse, to believe the interpretations and judgments of the negative affirmations. Begin these affirmations with "I Am Not..."

6) Affirming "A Life in Pieces" will erase the effects, and therefore the existence, of the black hole, because the brain can only hold one thought at a time. Therefore, we all have a choice: the black hole or peace?

Do I dare to dream that every man and woman will choose peace? Do I dare to dream of children living happily and equally with adults? Do I dare to dream of peaceful connections with mutual respect and liking, of all religions, cultures, men and women? Children go beyond dreaming and believe this can happen, with some children as young as pre-teens involved in the process of implementing, then running, programs themselves to solidify more peaceful homes, schools, and even countries. We need to be guided by them, because their solutions are so simple, with few rules and regulations. Children must trust it is the human spirit that will lead this world naturally to peace, because they realize adults cannot. Dream with me and choose peace. We all deserve it.

Chapter Ten

Seeds to Humanity vs. Seeds of Destruction

Share with me now, then implement, the words that intensify our natural abilities to live "as one." Together, they create what I believe to be the true meaning of humanity: virtues shared by a collective group of people joined by all that is excellent.

GOOD   HAPPY   BEAUTY
EAGER   LOVE/WANT
CHEERFUL   CHOICE
FRIEND/PARTNER   TALK/COMMUNICATE
FAIR   HELP
BRIGHT   REMEMBER

Share with me now, then eliminate, the words that destroy happiness, calm, and ultimately the chance for peace.

BAD   ANNOYING   FORGETFUL
DISRESPECTFUL   MEAN/MALICIOUS
RESENTFUL   SELFISHLY NEEDY
UNSUPPORTIVE   UN-COOPERATIVE
BIASED   HYPER/DISRUPTIVE
ANGRY/VENGEFUL   SELFISH/UNFEELING

I define these words to the best of my ability so you can feel the genuine truth found in each, but I want you to understand that the meanings transcend what can be put on paper. They will touch deep within the soul as you experience their growth. These words, which fill the spirit with happy and safe feelings, will guide your actions from the heart. All will be different. All will be calm. Listen now, and feel examples of how I believe children would respond to positive and negative affirmations regarding their innate goodness.

CHAPTER ELEVEN

"GROWN-UPS, I WANT TO RESPOND."

I AM GOOD

I AM good, kind, heartful, and warm.

I know this because I want to care for others when they are sick.

I am concerned with how I act and try to be easy to get along with.

I know this because I follow rules that I am emotionally and physically able to. I attempt to follow every rule, even if it is not possible for me to comply with all of them.

I am capable of knowing the difference between right and wrong; I can feel it inside.

I know this because I will not strike out at anyone for no reason. I want to be respected.

I am strong in many outstanding and excellent qualities. I feel and acknowledge them with pride.

I know this because I glow in delight when others recognize them within my heart. I am sad and confused when others do not. I am helpless to understand others' dislike towards me. I would understand this feeling if I had bad qualities, but thankfully... .

I AM NOT BAD

I AM NOT a brat, nor am I a bad person with a wicked, evil character who is morally reprehensible.

I know this because I do not understand what this means. How can I be this way if I do not know how to act as a wicked, evil, and morally reprehensible person? I do not like the name "brat," because it is insinuating that I am spoiled, impolite, and annoying. These cannot exist because I am good and selfless.

I am not disapproving, thus needing your censure.

I know this because my heart tells me not to hurt others and not to be difficult. I want to tell you that I know you have misinterpreted my actions. I want to disapprove of this name calling and I am justified in doing so.

I am not sinful.

I know this because I AM KIND. I cannot be morally virtuous and morally evil at the same time. I want you to change your description of me, because if you believe I am a brat and I am bad, you will not find joy in my presence.

I AM EAGER

I AM eager, keen, and enthusiastic.

I know this because my tummy laughs inside where no one can see.

I am sometimes intense with feeling because of something fun I did or because of something that happened to me. I feel this way when I go to the water park for the day or get invited to a birthday party.

I know this because I am about to explode with excitement and am unable to sit still. It is hard to think about what you are teaching me, but I try.

I am sensitive.

I know this because my sensitivity in times that are tormenting (for example, abuse and/or condemnation towards me) creates fear and confusion in me. I am scared when my parents will not stop hitting me and causing me to bleed. This pain makes it hard for me to obey in school. If you knew, I hope you would not yell so much. Your yelling makes me more sensitive and I have an even harder time focusing.

I am earnest and serious with intention—like when I try and share an exciting story or ask you questions about something I am curious about.

I know this because I am sincere in this feeling. I feel it deep within my body and I have a hard time controlling this emotion. I am not disobeying. I am feeling a great urgency to share and to question, making it difficult to calm down. I am not trying to make it hard for you to teach or parent me.

I am expectant, knowing or anticipating something is about to happen.

I know this because my mind is thinking about what is coming next and I have a hard time listening. I can feel my tummy tickle as I wait for things and occasions, like a fieldtrip, Christmas present, or graduation. It is natural for all people to feel excited about an upcoming special event or a surprise.

I am dispassionate, just, and can find calm.

I know this because I am fair and I want to make things easy for you. I am concerned about my conduct and want it to be "right."

I AM NOT DISRESPECTFUL

I AM NOT dispassionate (another meaning, different from the above) and totally lacking personal feeling, unaffected by passion.

I know this because I love discovering and investigating how the world works. I feel passionate about everything, and that is why I am sometimes hyper and I interrupt. I am curious about everything. I also feel the heartache of others and this affects me personally.

I am not disrespectful. I do not complain to intentionally make you mad at me.

I know this because I will not lose my temper or be unjustly dissatisfied and resentful. I am kind and considerate of others, meaning I cannot be disrespectful.

I am not disruptive, intentionally interrupting you and disobeying your rules.

I know this because I would have to consciously plan such behavior. As a young child, I am not capable of this process. As I get older, I will not intentionally break any rules I understand and could obey, because such behavior comes from an empty, uncaring heart, unconcerned about the consequences of one's actions. That is not me.

I am not needing a label because I am hyper.

I know this because I am a child, naturally hyper and curious about everything in my world; anxious to find answers to all that is unknown to me. Being hyper is not bad. I will be calmer in a happy environment where I am liked. I will be more hyper and anxious if you do not like me.

I AM CHEERFUL

I AM cheerful, in laughing spirits, pleasant, and bright.

I know this because I feel like I have to shout out loud to settle down, as I feel excitement through my whole body. I am smiling all over! I feel hyper in my happiness! I cannot sit still! I talk lots and I am loud! I love it!

I am ungrudging, willing, and pleased—giving joy to those around me.

I know this because I feel no insult or injury when you ask me, the cheerful one, to comply. I do, if I can.

I am losing this cheerful spirit, feeling indignant and insulted.

I know this because some expectations are not reasonable and, with reason, I get offended. At these times, I feel anger that is justified.

I am sometimes insulted and angry when my actions are misinterpreted as harmful.

I know this because I am in laughing spirits, pleasant, kind, and warm, therefore I cannot be deliberately harmful. I get justifiably angry when I must repress my opposition to this injustice.

I AM NOT RESENTFUL

I AM NOT deliberately resentful for no reason.

I know this because I am not selfish and I do not feel sorry for myself. If I seem to resent your behavior towards me, it is legitimate. You have insulted me and it feels uncomfortable and unfair. I would like it to change.

I am not grudging or vengefully angry.

I know this because I am not capable of feeling or understanding what this means. I do not want to feel this way. I am not out to get anyone. If you see me as vengeful, you have misinterpreted me and my actions.

I am not displeasing or offensive to be around.

I know this because I listen as well as I can and obey when I can. This is because I want every one to like me. If I am hyper, tell yourself I am cheerful, not displeasing. If I seem resentful, understand it as legitimate and ask me why I feel this way. You will be more accepting of me, if you are not feeling unpleasant in my presence.

I AM A FRIEND AND PARTNER

I AM attached to others, feeling affection in my heart.

I know this because I love to reach out to people who are sad. I am proud to help my partners.

I am partners with all persons in my life.

I know this because I am proud to share at work time, when we are playing, and when we build nice things together. I want to keep doing this. There is cooperation when I respect my partners, because then they respect me. We may not be friends who share an intimate bond, but not everyone has to be my friend. Adults are not friends with everyone.

I am on moral and upright terms with others.
I know this because in my heart I know I am kind.

I am productive with others.

I know this because others want to work with me and are pleased to follow my direction. Sometimes they want to copy my kind deeds and/or my intelligent masterpieces. You can too!

I AM NOT UNSUPPORTIVE

I AM NOT controlling.

I know this because I do not want to, or feel like I can, deliberately dominate playtime. I am not a bossy friend. I may be a little egocentric when I am younger, a natural tendency in little children, but I will not hurt anyone because I am kind. I can share because I am fair. Do not worry if I do not share. I am not unjust, nor unkind, so I am not doing it to hurt someone's feelings.

I am not restraining, holding others back from their choices and making them do what I want them to.

I know this because my partners would not be happy in my company if I demanded such control. My partners willingly play with me, so they are happy to be in my presence.

I am not dominating, more valuable or powerful than my friends.

I know this because I have friends who would not play with me if I were.

I AM FAIR

I AM equal in relationships, wanting all sides to be alike.

I know this because I want to have friends like everyone else. Being fair is a way to have and keep friends.

I am favoring no one, not even myself.

I know this because I enjoy the process of sharing, even helping my schoolmates keep track of whose turn will be next. This makes me proud.

I am fair, legitimately seeking a reason for sharing and turn-taking.

I know this because my heart tells me when I need to share. If there is a legitimate reason for my turn to end, this will happen. If

I can/should, without guilt, continue with my play, I will. Do not worry, because you know I am kind and not hurtful. I am too proud of my moral character to be favorable only to myself or to my friends.

I am concerned about the decencies of behavior, like being fair.

I know this because I want the approval of my parents, family, and teachers. I want to feel adequate as a person, and I want others to remember I am kind.

I am aware that all my partners/friends are compassionate; I am reminded often by my parents and my teachers.

I know this because I feel these common qualities among my classmates. I do not look at differences; I look at heart.

I AM NOT BIASED

I AM NOT biased and racist.

I know this because the act of disliking someone due to race, gender, religion, et cetera, is very intentional, not something that I can plan, or want, to engage in. I wish you knew this, because there are days when I decide not to play with a particular classmate(s), or my brother or sister, and I am not being mean or biased. I know who it is I want to play with and, just like an adult, I have the ability to say no without being biased. My heart will tell me if I am causing hurt towards another because I am kind and intuitive. I need you to relax, stop obsessing over the need to have things work out "your way."

*I want to stress, and repeat, an important point. It could very likely be adults' obsessive emphasis on teaching feelings and emotions, like "sad" and "mad," that are causing children to scream discrimination and unfair treatment by friends and partners as often as they do. There would be few complications in a child's interaction with another if indignation and hurt feelings were not taught. Children are simple people filled with humility, respect, and modesty. Children are capable of making choices without your interference. It is interesting that some parents make the choice to reprimand children when they themselves yell at each other. At the same time that children are requested to respect each other, share and be kind, mom and dad are fighting. A very young child can sense this hypocrisy. This is unfair and biased.

I AM BRIGHT

I AM BRIGHT, radiant, vivid, and brilliant.

I know this because I want to shine for everyone around me and show them how smart I am.

I am witty and clever in perception.

I know this because my senses and my mind make me aware of others' intentions toward me. Sometimes I wish I were not so aware, because I cannot learn when I am with you. I can tell you do not like me.

I am insightful and keen in understanding.

I know this because I behave differently around those who bully me and those who do not.

I am able to understand the motivation behind my behaviors.

I know this because I have been so confused by your misinterpretation of my intentions. I want you to understand me. If you misinterpret my actions, please ask me what my intention was, and I will tell you. I do understand my behavior. Sometimes the intention behind my behavior is to tell you to stop being unfair and mean. Sometimes it is you who is hurting my feelings and scaring me. I need you to listen.

I AM NOT ANGRY OR VENGEFUL

I AM NOT angry, in the sense that I want revenge.

I know this because I am glad, meaning I am showing and feeling cheerfulness, remember? We have already determined that I love to be cheerful, getting along with others, cooperating so I am liked. Therefore, if I am angry, understand that there is something wrong and this emotion is justified. I have no desire to intentionally cause any stress or frustration, because this will work to my disadvantage as you will dislike me.

I am not dead on the inside, showing lack of feeling and sensory understanding.

I know this because I can clearly understand the feeling of safety as it creates a sense of calm. I am happy and rambunctious, waking up in the morning with joyful anticipation of the upcoming events of the day. Sadly, some of you have mistaken me for one who does not feel, therefore you are not silent, nor cautious, about showing your dislike towards me. You are often angry at me and I do not know why. You do not think I feel what you are doing to me, but I feel your dislike through my whole body and I am afraid of you. Sometimes I wish I did not feel.

I AM HAPPY

I AM pleasing and gratifying to be around.

I know this because **I AM** funny. I make my family laugh all the time. My mom and dad are very pleased to be in my company.

I am enjoyable to be around and suitable for others to accept as a friend.

I know this because I gladly piece into another person's mind and heart. I enjoy and accept the ideas of others, and I want others to enjoy me and my ideas.

I am lucky, and I bring luck to others.

I know this because I feel lucky and special when experiencing joy, especially when and where I least expect it. I like surprising those around me with unforeseen fun and surprises. I like to make them laugh. I want my friends/partners, teachers and parents to feel lucky to have me in their lives.

I am fortunate when my heart fills with happiness.

I know this because I feel so relaxed and unafraid. Those around me do not have to put any direct effort into making me happy, as the circumstances surrounding me fill me with cheer. This is genuine fortune and happiness.

I AM NOT ANNOYING

I AM NOT a persistent trouble maker, irritating, or disturbing.

I know this because I do not intentionally plan to irritate anyone; it is not worth it. This will make you dislike me and it is me who pays the biggest price for your negative attention towards me. My parents, my family, the teachers in my school, and my fellow classmates will all come to see me as a problem.

I am not problematic, or bothersome.

I know this because my mind cannot determine, especially at a young age, what it entails to be a problem, manipulative, aggravating, annoying, or a super-brat. The problem is I am mislabeled. The tragedy is that I am labeled at all. The impossible truth is that you have called me bothersome and problematic, even when I was only two. I am only a child. I do not know what you are telling me. I know you are unhappy around me. I find this problematic to my well-being.

I AM LOVE

I AM profoundly tender, from the depths of my being.

I know this because I am affectionate towards others and really enjoy the company of my family and friends. I feel so much.

I am gentle and moved to sympathy.

I know this because I love to be touched and touch back. It allows me to bond and I feel safe. I feel anxious and scared for, and sympathize with, my friend or partner who is yelled at. I am afraid when the yelling is directed towards me, especially when it happens on a regular basis. I wish my parents and the teachers could empathize with this. I want a gentle hug and a sympathetic relationship.

I am wanting, and am working towards, personal attachments.

I know this because these attachments make me feel calm and I have a passion for learning when the environment allows the growth of warm attachments. I learn and socialize better in loving and mutually respectful relationships. I will do everything I can to ensure such relationships. I am so desiring of safe, personal attachments that I am sad when I see you warm up to children you think are appropriately behaved, but ignore me except when you have something negative to tell me. I feel detached and I try to make you like me, but I am not like these other children. I am more hyper, excitable, and curious; it is part of my nature, but I am as equally loving and kind.

I AM NOT MEAN OR MALICIOUS

I AM NOT bad-tempered or ignoble, with mean motives.

I know this because I have been paying attention to all the qualities I possess, and it is not possible to be mean when I possess all the qualities of beauty. Sensitive, warm, and fair cannot exist with a mean, dishonorable character. This is why I do not understand your dislike towards me. Sometimes it feels like you are mean to me, and I do not understand why you want to feel this way.

I do not want to seek revenge when I am angry.

I know this because when I am angry inside, I feel insulted and abused. I am overwhelmed by the constant nagging towards me; I never do anything right in your eyes. When I scream out with injustice, I am angry and it is my way of saying "too much." I need you to stop and examine what you are doing to me. I do not want the stress and disloyalty of revenge. That will get us nowhere.

I AM WANT

I AM wishing on a star, wanting and longing for your care.

I know this because I am calm around those who like me and are fair and just. I love to be liked. I love to be loved.

I am needing you to understand my intentions so we can get along better.

I know this because it is the misunderstanding of things I do that make you upset, thus making me sad and confused. I want to cooperate and help you understand why I act the way I do. This will create a more affectionate bond between us. I need to be able to share my feelings: if I hurt inside, if I am afraid, or if I am excited.

I am understanding that I need to follow your rules and behave the best I can.

I know this because I am concerned about you and your feelings. I want to make things easy for you.

I am desiring, possessing affection and joy.

I know this because, just as you are pleased that your heart feels affection and joy, so am I. I want to share these feelings. Please enjoy what I have to give.

I am urgently requesting your attention when I have been hurt by an adult. I am serious in my need for your understanding when this happens to me.

I know this because I want to cry and I sometimes pray for a new life.

I AM NOT SELFISHLY NEEDY

I AM NOT intentionally difficult, in need of virtue.

I know this because I cannot understand how my heart can be difficult, nor do I understand why I am not kind and fair when I am born. How can you see me as intentionally hard to deal with or get along with?

I am not wanting too much, nor am I selfishly needy.

I know this because I feel safe and justified in my requests for help and attention. I do not ask for, or need more than is necessary. I try not to ask for too much because that upsets you and I get into trouble. But, as a child, I sometimes do not know where and when to stop.

I AM ABLE TO CHOOSE

I AM choosing to be kind, fair and warm.

I know this because I have the feelings that come to me when experiencing warm connections. I want to avoid emotions that cause anxiety, frustration, and despair.

I am choosing to be easy to get along with.

I know this because I have one of two options: behave in a way that causes negative emotions, or cooperate respectfully and easily to bring happiness and harmony. I choose happiness. I am perceptive, so I understand the difference between the two. I know there is only one choice because they cannot both exist together.

I am excited when the activity, book, or the game that I prefer is chosen by the teacher. I feel special.

I know this because I feel excited about my choice. It is fun to experience something I am very interested in and I love to have my friends experience this with me. It is okay to get what we want sometimes. It makes children smile and feel lucky.

I AM NOT UNCOOPERATIVE

I AM NOT disagreeable or unwilling.

I know this because I have no negative feelings toward you, or your activity, when you make a choice I did not prefer. I am upset that, again, my choice was unimportant. I sometimes wish my preference would be considered; this would make me happy, like it makes you or anyone else happy.

I am not caring only about myself.

I know this because I will lose friends and partners if I do, and I do not want this to happen. As a young child, it may seem as though I am intentionally dominating an activity or holding onto a toy, not willing to share. Please understand it is not intentional. Young children live through a stage of egocentricity that they will grow out in time. It is natural, not intentional, and there is no desire to do anyone harm.

I am not egotistical or conceited, valuing only what is of interest to me.

I know this because there is no reason for me to be so empty of feelings and emotions; no benefits will be realized as I will have no friends, and you and I will have a frustrating relationship. It is because of your interpretation of my thoughts and behavior, or because you do not like me, that makes you think I want what is of value solely to me.

93

I AM CAPABLE OF COMMUNICATING AND I WANT TO TALK
I AM excited to share my ideas. I want to impart information to you as I am learning about my new surroundings. I am eager to ask you questions about things I am curious about.

I know this because my tummy tickles and my heart races when words want to fly from my mouth. I enjoy the opportunity to share. It is in this way I invite you into my heart and my character.

I am expressive.

I know this because I am able to put thoughts into words and turn them into meaningful statements and conversation. I love to express these. Thank you when you respect me and let me speak, and thank you when you pay attention to what I have to say. I respect the fact that I can wait if you tell me we can share at a better time. Giving respect gets respect.

I am able, and I want, to express thoughts and feelings easily and effectively.

I know this because, at the moment of highest excitement or sensitivity, my thoughts are clear in my mind. What comes with my clear mind is a queasy stomach because I am excited to express these thoughts when they are most vivid. At that moment, I feel it is easiest for me to put my thoughts into words. It is hard when you tell me the time is not right; I try all the time to respect that. I do not want to make things difficult, but sometimes I forget what I want to share if I have to wait. Sometimes though, I would love to share and I need to share. This would make me so happy.

I AM NOT HYPER (in a "bad" way) OR DISRUPTIVE
I AM NOT interrupting and rude.

I know this because I am kind. I do not want to disrupt the class and have everyone mad at me. If I interrupt, my excitement and curiosity are just too overwhelming. I will try and stop out of respect. I understand that if I want you to listen to me, I must show the same respect and make it easy for you to teach all the students.

I am not disrespectful or hyper in an unreasonable way.

I know this because I am curious, meaning my sensory system, including my insides, my nerves, my brain, and all that makes me eager, sensitive, and curious, feels like exploding with excitement. You do not appreciate, understand, or think about this, therefore you see my intentions incorrectly. You try to silence and calm me ("de-hyper") me, thus you try to control me. You cannot change how I am, or any child is wired, no matter how much you try to control our behavior. Sadly, the more you control, the more out-of-control we get. This is a fact with adults as well.

I AM A HELPER

I AM wanting and able to assist others who need my help.

I know this because I am kind, concerned for others, and I worry if they are having trouble. I feel when someone else is in need, I desire to relieve some of their stress. Empathy and sympathy are two valuable qualities I possess.

I am willing to help others when needed.

I know this because I am so proud after I come to the aid of others, creating an urge to experience this feeling again. I want you to pay more attention when I help my classmates because the act of helping exposes kindness and selflessness. Please do not take this for granted.

I am willing to help relieve the pain and distress of others.

I know this because I feel sad and afraid when someone is suffering or being hurt by another person. I do not want just to stand by. I am empathetic. I can feel their heartache.

I AM NOT SELF-CENTERED OR UNFEELING

I AM NOT empty inside, incapable of seeing when another person needs my assistance.

I know this because I understand when I should, and can, help another who is distressed about an incident or anxious because of a difficult task. You do not have to expect this of me, or ask me. My heart will guide me. It would help us have a better, more calming and respectful relationship if you recognized giving times, emphasizing kind deeds with statements like: "You are so helpful, you came to your partner's aid," "You are very bright, understanding your partner needed help" and "You are very helpful to me when you are patient."

I am not willing to help only my friends and not others.

I know this because I feel the same empathy towards all who are in need. I am also fair, meaning I am unbiased, favoring no one over another, especially in times of need.

I AM ABLE TO REMEMBER

I AM able to remember all these words that build confidence in myself and those around me.

I know this because my heart is growing with pride. Speaking often of my virtuous character is permanently planting these truthful qualities within me. I cannot forget words of excellence, especially when they are spoken far more often than words from the black hole. I want to remember. My mind and heart will remember. I will thrive in your care!

I am confident that I will remember these words of beauty. They have an intense impact on me.

I know this because the ability to remember is connected to what is happening to the brain and when people are in atmospheres of calm, created by the continual use of these affirmations, there is a relaxed feeling within, and the brain is able to learn in a more memorable way. In this tranquil atmosphere, you will remember the beauty of my true character and hold these pleasant memories of me forever.

I am able to remember your attitude towards me and the impact it has on my attitude and disposition.

I know this because there are so many days I feel sad and confused because you treat me unfairly. I have lost my energy. Teacher, I am affected by your behavior towards me even before I get dressed for school. I am frightened when my mom wakes me up for another day because I do not want to go to school. Mom and dad, I am afraid and anxious when I get ready to go home from school because I remember how you make me feel unsafe. My body reacts to indifference and injustice, especially when I can never speak out for my rights. I do not want to go home. Everyone, please remember to be kind to me.

I AM NOT FORGETFUL

I AM NOT an empty shell, able to ignore your mistreatment of me.

I know this because I remember the words from the black hole you use to describe my character. I hear you say them often around others, like my classmates and friends.

I am not intentionally forgetting, nor am I stupid.

I know this because my memory retains thoughts of your dislike for me and it is this that affects my ability to recall the information that you teach me. I have a more difficult time remembering the class lessons and I also have a more difficult time remembering your rules, consequences, and solutions when you are mean to me. This behavior, and these attitudes towards me, work against what you are trying to achieve. Not only is my learning affected, but also my ability to be socially acceptable. I become more impulsive and desperate.

I AM BEAUTY

I AM filled with qualities that bring intense emotion and sensation, providing pleasure to all those around me.

I know this because I experience this intense aesthetic pleasure from others and I know I want to give back what I am given. I feel this grow inside my heart and I know I will explode if I do not release it into the lives of those around me. I am emotional and sensational. I am happy.

I am sincere and heartfelt; deep, not superficial.

I know this because I am guided by my innate virtues. My actions are built through intent that grows from a free spirit and mine is free to love and be kind. Therefore my intentions are not harmful, selfish or disrespectful. I am fake and superficial if I grow into the life you think I should have, and the personality/character you think I am and should be. This eliminates sincerity and creates a very superficial world, existing by, and for, the control and needs of others. There is always someone controlling another's actions, and children are always controlled.

I am remarkably noteworthy, excellent with outstanding qualities.

I know this because I have now experienced many other word definitions describing, in minute detail, me! How can anyone think differently!

I AM NOT...

I AM NOT going to defend myself anymore! I am no longer afraid, because I have faith in myself and those around me who know that....

I AM KIND!

I AM FAIR!

I AM EAGER!

I AM CHEERFUL!

I AM A FRIEND AND PARTNER!

I AM BEAUTY!

I AM ALL THAT YOU NEED ME TO BE!

I AM ME!

I AM ALL I NEED TO BE!

Chapter Twelve

Success

Readers, I now invite you to live what you have learned from this journey. No longer do you have to imagine a world empowered and impassioned by simple and humble adults, striving for genuine peace and equality for all of mankind. This is a successful conclusion of "A Life in Pieces." No more do children have to long for relationships with adults who possess benevolent qualities that they share with, and intensify in, all children. Likewise, adults no longer need fret over the fear of children running amok, ruthless, and violent. No more longing and no more fear, as "A Life in Pieces" engages the innate virtues of children from the moment they are born, successfully instilling kindness and compassion for eternity.

I conclude with my promise to all children. It is my hope that all adults who become members of change will live by these words:

I Promise

I will not take anything for granted and see you as bad. I will not assume you cannot make decisions about moral responsibility or that you are intentionally defiant and unwilling. I will not see you as unreasonable, interruptive, deviant, or manipulative. I will always see you as:

Cheerful, giving comfort and joy;

Eager, earnest, and enthusiastic, possessing the ability to be patient;

Friendly and kind, wanting to assist others;

Good, with a high quality of moral excellence;

Helping, as you make situations less unpleasant for your friends/partners;

Bright and radiant, brilliant and splendid; and
Fair and unbiased, free from dishonesty.

With respect to you, I will help you:
Choose, with your guidance, as there are many possibilities, preferences and desires, and I would like to help you choose the safer and wiser ones.

Understand happy, delightful, and fortunate, while we identify your unselfish wants, which are your desires and needs.

Remember and retain mental impressions and instructions to recall to the mind.

I want you to help me remember to love with profound tenderness, warmth, and attachment.

I will always remind myself to:
Examine, inspect, and scrutinize how I can improve your life and prepare you for the future. I will observe, test, and investigate; and

Analyze and separate into parts to determine the essential features of problems so I can hopefully identify causes and possible results.

Children, be proud of yourself! You give me a great sense of pleasure and satisfaction. In your presence, I am highly glorified!